My Vice is Verses

My Vice Is Verses

Bernard Yaeger

BRUNSWICK

Copyright © 2000 by Bernard Yaeger

All rights reserved under International and Pan-American Copyright Conventions. No part of this book may be reproduced in any form or by any means, electronic or mechanical, including photocopying or by any informational storage or retrieval systems, without written permission from the author and the publisher, except by a reviewer who may quote brief passages in a review.

Cover theme from the Rubaiyat of OMAR KHAYYAM
"A Book of Verses underneath the Bough
A Jug of Wine, a Loaf of Bread-and Thou"

Library of Congress Cataloging-in-Publication Data

Yaeger, Bernard, 1922-
My vice is verses / Bernard Yaeger.--1st ed.
p. cm.
ISBN 1-55618-187-6 (alk. paper)
I. Title

PS3575.A27 M9 2000
811'.6--dc21

00-037901

Some of these poems have been previously self-published by the author under the title Gnome Poems. Others have been reworked and included for one complete volume of poetry by the author.

First Edition

Published in the United States of America

by

Brunswick Publishing Corporation

1386 Lawrenceville Plank Road
Lawrenceville, Virginia 23868
1-800-336-7154

Acknowledgements

I wish to acknowledge the invaluable suggestions, positive criticism and moral support provided by the Poets of the Vineyard of Santa Rosa, California. Their words of encouragement helped me to bridge the uncertainty that new poets feel when they first submit their literary efforts to other members of the poetic fraternity for critique. Their comments, suggestions and critiques were most helpful.

Table of Contents

Section Four — My Name Is Adam

Section Five — Religious Poetry

Section Six — Death and Dying

Section Seven — Humorous Poems

Section Eight — Poetry and Writing

Section Nine — Patriotic Poems

Section Ten — Warfare

Section Eleven — Political Poems

Section Twelve — Law and the Courts

Section Seventeen — Miscellaneous

Section One

Life Reflections

Our Destiny

My voice speaks out as best it can
From here inside the mind of man
An impression I would like to share
That we are on the way somewhere.

I hear response from those outside
Who hear my voice and then confide
That others, too, along with me
Are curious about our destiny.

With philosophers we try to find
The mystery of all humankind.
We feel and think and then expect
To get answers with our intellect.

With holy men to serve as guides
We study books where faith resides
And hear what ancients have to say
Then expect faith to show the way.

With scientists we probe and test
And search for limits in our quest
To find the facts which should provide
The truth which cannot be denied.

We search from atoms to the skies
Until reluctantly we realize
That there is more than we can see
When we comprehend that destiny.

We know that there is more to life
Than unremitting toil and strife.
We sense there is a different goal
That finds response in every soul.

So hand-in-hand we struggle toward
The end that is our life's reward,
And trust that love and harmony
Will help us reach that destiny.

As together, we, in darkness grope
With confidence in faith and hope,
That one day we will understand
Our journey to that distant land.

Son of Adam

Since Adam ran
That's why I can
And I can swim
Just like him!

If Adam flew
I could too!
When Adam erred
I concurred.

Here Within

I sense that I am here within
Inside this flesh and bone,
Inside this solitary cell
Which is my earthly home.

And locked am I inside this cell
Inside this time and space
Inside this ever-changing world
Which is my designated place.

Here from inside my single cell
Through senses out I see
To become aware of another world
That I must call reality.

This world outside my cell of skin
Yields not my demands upon it
I cannot force the outside world
To grant what and when I want it.

My senses see a finite space
With more space beyond to see
Which reaches to an unknown end
That I can call infinity.

The world outside that I can sense
In which I have a place
Is just another cell I find
For trapped am I in time and space.

My time on earth is one small cell
Inside time's total span
Of times before and yet to come
That encompass all of man.

The pass of time I cannot change
Nor can I delay its paces
Time once passed is now no more
And I cannot replay its traces.

The past is gone by time's decree
The morrow's ever distant
Today and now I live my life
At time's pace most insistent.

Yet here inside this hollow skull
My memory has not perished
I can recall the shadowy scenes
Of times once lived and cherished.

Though I may yearn for other years
Or for previous times and places,
I cannot find escape from now
Or from time's relentless paces.

For held am I in time's domain
And whether I hate or love it
The here and now of every day
I must live each minute of it.

And though I may in fancy fly
From out this fleshy prison
To escape my place in time and space
It is never but illusion.

For trapped am I inside this time
Inside this skin and bone
Inside this cell of living flesh
Which I can call my own.

When life seems long and difficult
And escape is what I covet
I still cherish life which binds me here
And above all else I love it.

Yet when I yearn to escape from here
Fearful am I to achieve it
For though I may not like my lot
Fearful am I to leave it.

For everyone within his soul
Must often wonder why
That everyone must live a life
Then everyone must die.

For compelled I am to ever age
And with nature's laws comply
To continue living all my life
Then doomed I am to die.

For I must die ere I escape
And death is filled with wonder
For what lies beyond I do not know
And that "unknown" I ponder.

The Lot of Life

I have enjoyed many pleasures of living
Many blessings of life I've received
Yet reluctantly came I into this world
And more reluctantly yet will I leave.

I have enjoyed the exuberance of springtime
When the new life of nature springs forth
I have danced with delight in the moonlight
When living seems at its full worth.

I have basked with delight in the sunshine
And felt the sharp sting of the cold.
I have gloried in my youthful vigor
And have suffered the chills of the old.

I have enjoyed the warmth of the fire
When the blizzards of winter have come
I have battled the forces of nature
And enjoyed all the comforts of home.

I have labored in the heat of the wheat fields
When the work of the day must be done.
I've been cooled by thirst quenching water
After sweating in the hot summer's sun.

I have enjoyed the freshness of morning
Before the day's work has begun
I've exulted in the work I've accomplished
And my rest when the day's work is done.

I have enjoyed the view from the mountain
I have suffered in the depths of despair
I have enjoyed all the beauties of nature
And grieved when they were no longer there.

I have thirsted for the waters of wisdom
And hungered for the nourishment of truth
I have searched for the pleasures of beauty
And have mourned for the health of my youth.

I have struggled with my animal urges
And with all the other conflicts of life
I have battled with nature's temptations
And have fought with my brothers in strife.

My feet have been bruised by the cobbles
My flesh has been rent by the thorn
My bones have broken when I stumbled
And my skin has been abraded and torn.

I have felt the debilitation of illness
And suffered the discomfort of pain
I have fought off the effects of the virus
And regained my health time and again.

I have suffered the agonies of migraine
When my head has been throbbing with ache
My internal condition has oft been awry
When my vigor was upset with an ague.

My nose has been filled with congestion
My lungs can't get the air that they need
My eyes have oft itched and been reddened
Due to dust and the pollen from weeds.

I have feared all the forces of nature
I fear storm and tornado and flood
And when the ground trembles beneath me
I fear the many forces not understood.

For my body is the body of mankind
And my spirit is the spirit of love
I exist as one unit of nature
Under the benevolent eye from above.

For I am one cell among many
That Nature controls with her plan
And Heaven is watching the struggle
That is the life and the fate of man.

Ancestors

She had the virtues
So Eve believed
But as for faults
Adam had 'em!

SECTION TWO:

Living a Life

Rules To Live By

The mothers I admire most today
Are those who teach their children how to play
The game of life by learning useful tools
And learning how to live life by the rules.
For rules that children learn at mother's knee
Are rules that they will live by constantly.
Because in adult life the penalty
For breaking rules is used consistently.
The child must learn and clearly understand
He should not try to get the upper hand
And win by ways that are not legally
Permitted in adult society.
Then he can live a life that grants reward
To those who get ahead by working hard.

Horse Sense

Little children
So 'tis said
Don't have horse sense
Inside their head.

But when you look
At what adults do
That can be said
For some grown-ups too!

Praises

When I first got my wooden blocks
I built a tower to admire
But when I showed it to my Dad
He said, "Go build it higher."

I remember all through grade school
I tried and tried to be
A student worthy of my Dad
And make my father proud of me.

Then one time I thought I had
I got an "A" in math
I showed it proudly to my Dad
But he said, "Go take your bath."

And once again in high school
The time I got all "A's"
When I showed my card to father
He said, "Don't tell me you want praise."

Now that I am a father
If my son wants me to praise him
I will be generous with applause
Because I know just how to raise him.

For praise is the incentive
For everyone who strives
To do the things they ought to do
To live healthy, productive lives.

Time For Fun

When I was just a little kid
I had no cares to shun
So I just played around a lot
Because everything was FUN.

But when I hit my teenage years
Dad said, "There's work that must be done
After you've finished growing up
There'll be lots of time for FUN."

I swore when I was old enough
There is nothing I would shun
I'd get my fill of drugs and drink
And enjoy all kinds of FUN.

Then Dad sent me off to college
Where I was always on the run
To keep my grades respectable
Before I could start having FUN.

But when I got my first good job
I had to work from sun to sun
Even though I had ready money
There was little time for FUN.

As soon as I hit forty
When they say life's just begun
The bills for home and family
Stopped me from having FUN.

So I tried again at fifty
And again at fifty-one
But folks said, "Build your nest egg"
There's still lots of time for FUN.

When I reached age sixty-five
And my retirement had begun
Alas! the sad truth was, I found,
I was too old to have much FUN.

But now I'm in my seventies
And my my life's work has been done
I find that over all the years
Just plain living is what's FUN.

Western Serenade

Coyotes howl
A single vowel
Why they do it?
There's nothing to it.

They see the moon
And start to croon.
If it's love they want
I wish they'd hunt!

Life Stages

When I was in my younger years
I had to go to school
To learn about my future life
It was the established rule.

I had to learn the things I'd need
When I became a grown adult
For effective preparation
Means a successful grown result.

I did have lots of time to play
In boyish games and such,
But I yearned to be a grown-up
Which I wanted very much.

There were lots of things I wanted
But they said wait until you're grown
Now be happy with the joys of youth
Because each age has its own.

When I reached the age of twenty-one
And for many years ensuing
I enjoyed my grown-up privileges
But much work needed doing.

So many times in forty years
That I was a working man
I yearned for carefree living
Which was my desired plan.

I looked ahead to my golden years
When my working life was over
So I could lie abed each morning
And live my life in clover.

I scrimped and saved and struggled
To acquire wealth and money
So after the age of sixty-five
I could live on milk and honey.

Then at last it finally came
The day I had dreamed about
I retired from my occupation
And work I could live without.

I enjoy my new found leisure
And my carefree days from strife
This is the life worth living
This is the rewarding life.

But I know these days are numbered
So I look to the time ahead
Where there is predestined certainty
To the time when I'll be dead.

So I must look beyond this time
To my spirit's next existence
After I've reached the end of life
By natures grim insistence.

I now prepare for that next stage
And have gotten into the right condition
So when I cross that great divide
I can make a smooth transition.

Second Chance

My woes seemed insurmountable
My troubles caused me pain
I sought a way to find escape
And breathe carefree air again.

I tried the road less traveled
To see where it would go
But found it led to NOWHERE
A place I did not know.

I backtracked to the highway
To join the rushing throng
For on that bleak and lonely road
I sensed something very wrong.

I merged with the stream of travelers
Who struggle on their way
To meet the challenges of life
That must be faced each day.

For if I take the road less traveled
Loved ones are left behind
And causing pain to loved ones
Was never in my mind.

So now I trod the well-worn path
'Cause I no longer can pretend
There is escape on roads less traveled
That lead to an unknown end.

Section Three:

Love

Commitment

I wrote a letter to my love today
That said a lot of things I had to say.
I told her that my love would surely last
Until at least a thousand years had passed.
I told her she was always in my heart;
No pow'r on earth could pry us two apart.
I poured my love for her upon the page
And said my heart was at the breaking stage.
I asked her for her love in fair return
And begged her not my ardent love to spurn.
Then bravely asked this girl to be my wife
And made commitment that would last my life.
    And now I wait for her return reply.
    If she says no, then I will have to die!

Boyfriend

Salutated
Animated
Captivated
Intoxicated
Osculated
Fornicated
Impregnated
Repudiated
Abdicated!

Come To Me Beloved

Oh! Come to me beloved
And place your hand in mine
We'll unite our hearts together
So our lives will intertwine.

Then like the double helix
In the basic cell of life
We will bind our lives together
And be forever man and wife.

I'll leave my home and parents
To be always at your side,
We'll merge our dreams together
As the bridegroom and his bride.

For as once we met as strangers
Now we will live as friends
We'll overlook transgressions
And be quick to make amends.

We will blend our lives together
We will share a common name
We will have a common outlook
For our future's now the same.

Our hopes shall intermingle
Our fears we'll overcome
No more as lonely people
For we two shall be as one.

Your fears of life shall vanish
When I hold you in my arms
My love shall be protection
From life's worries, woes and harms.

I shall listen to your problems
All your troubles I will share
I'll provide advice and counsel
And you'll always know I care.

My compassion's your's in sorrow
When you're sick or feeling blue
You'll have my love and comfort
To restore good health to you.

I will greet you every morning
And pledge my trust to you
So our love will be rekindled
As we begin each day anew.

I will love you with great passion
My ardor shall not cool
I'll desire most to please you
It shall be my Golden Rule.

All my love to you I promise
Without any part reserved
And I pray to God in heaven
For our love to be preserved.

So to you my fond beloved
I pledge my true love to thee
And I'll be forever faithful
For life and all eternity.

Consider The Bride

Consider the bride on her wedding day
Consider the groom when they go away.

Consider their lives are now as one
Consider the union that has begun.

Consider adjustment as the price
Consider that love means sacrifice.

Consider that each is now restrained
Individual choice must now be reined.

Consider two lives that now must mesh
Consider their living in togetherness.

Consider the arguments they will have
Consider the promises they just gave.

Consider the life they left behind
Consider life now is a different kind.

Consider the differences they must solve
Consider how the marriage must evolve.

Consider how marriage is a human endeavor
Consider this union should last forever.

Consider how marriage is based on love.
That help is available from Above.

So dance and sing on this wedding day
Because Jesus at Cana showed the way.

Considering Birth

Consider the life of man my friend
Consider the beginning and the end.
Consider the urge that began it all
Consider how nature makes the call.

Consider a couple in the act of sex
Consider conception, so complex.
Consider that egg and sperm are twins
When they combine, new life begins.

Consider the babe in the mother's womb
It's snug and warm without much room
Consider it loves its pleasant ride
And knows not about the world outside.

Consider it hears its mother's heart
And know its life is a life apart.
Consider the babe in its cozy home
Is preparing itself for the life to come.

Then the day comes for the big transition
So it's maneuvered into the right position.
For the babe must leave the cozy nest
Because nature knows that birth is best.

Suddenly then, it's time for birth
The babe must take its place on earth.
So with push and shove and awesome force
The baby is born as a matter of course.

"I didn't want to be born" it cries
But without first breath the baby dies.
There in a strange and lighted place
The babe meets its mother face to face.

It hears its mother's cries of joy
She cares not if its girl or boy.
The babe is placed on its mother's arm
Then knows again it is safe from harm.

Consider the triumph that she knows
Consider the love and joy she shows
As she presses the baby to her breast
And feeds the child with nature's best.

Consider each birth as a grand event
And the newborn babe as heaven sent
Then try to claim there is no soul
Or to deny that God is in control.

Monthly Meetings

Some come, some don't
Some can't, some won't
We know, more could
We hope, more would!

Babies

Why are toddlers so appealing?
Why do babies look so sweet?
Why do newborns get attention
When you see them on the street?

Why do bear cubs seem so cuddly?
Why do kittens make one smile?
Why are frisky little puppies
So free and innocent of guile?

Why do the young of every species
Captivate with simple charm?
Why do calloused old policeman
Try to keep the young from harm?

Is this nature's way of giving
The added urge to stay alive
By making babies so appealing
She helps more of them to survive?

But then who wants an ugly baby?
Who would give it love and care?
If the young were not appealing
They'd be unwelcome everywhere!

Mother Nature knows the answer
Love for the young is the ideal
So all the members of the species
Will respond to the young's appeal.

So smile when you see a little baby
Express your love and gentleness
Then every baby will feel welcome
And enjoy this special friendliness.

Commiseration

When life ending
Friends attending
Can provide moral support
Comfort giving
To the living
Needing love when life is short.

Presence pleasing
Hands for squeezing
When the dreaded reaper comes
Pain progressing
Sudden stressing
Solace 'til the heart succumbs.

Love departed
Broken hearted
Future life looks cold and gray
Kinfolk kisses
Reminisces
Embraces take the pain away.

Fellow feeling
Helps in healing
Words that can the heart console
Thoughts inspired
Love required
Aid uplifting of the soul.

Ever grieving
After leaving
For the love that once was known
Lonely living
Fate forgiving
Whenever one goes on alone.

Constant caring
Selfless sharing
Put hearts in a healing mood
Not regretting
Nor forgetting
Expressing love's solicitude.

Time erases
Memory's traces
'Til the pain is felt no more
Grief decreases
Heart then ceases
Wishing life was like before.

Sorrow dwindling
Love rekindling
Can remove the mourning chill
Tender touching
Closely clutching
Shows that love the heart can fill.

Health and pleasure
Love and treasure
Enjoy the life that fate bestows
But if sorrow
Comes tomorrow
Stand steadfast 'til grieving goes.

Love's Lonely End

Since my love has gone away from me
My life is bleak and dreary
My wife has died after fifty years
And left me naught but pain and tears.
I mourn for her in memory still
There is a void I cannot fill.
  And though I know she's dead and gone
  I know that I must carry on
  For I must carry on.

The skies are always dark and gray
Since that sad day she went away.
The sun may shine and light the gloom
Flowers may grow and show their bloom
But there is no brightness in my life
Since that dark day I lost my wife.
  And though I know she's dead and gone
  I know that I must carry on
  For I must carry on.

The house is silent, dark and still
There is no warmth to chase the chill
My love is missing from my home
For I am living now alone.
A sadness has enveloped me
And loneliness is my company.
  And though I know she's dead and gone
  I know that I must carry on
  For I must carry on.

The conjugal bed is always cold
There is no one that I can hold
I find no comfort in her place
I find no solace in her embrace
So every night I turn and toss
As every night I mourn her loss.
   And though I know she's dead and gone
   I know that I must carry on
   For I must carry on.

My time to go has not yet come
My heart continues beating drum.
I see her there awaiting me
As she beckons to me silently.
I grieve and mourn in dark despair
Until the day I can join her there.
   I know my love is dead and gone.
   But I do not want to carry on
   For I cannot carry on.

Unfriendly Neighbor

When the neighbor's dog barks at 2 A.M.
And you phone him and complain
Don't expect a civil answer
When you must call him up again!

Section Four:

My Name is Adam

Mother

My name is Adam, and I am man
My life is lived in the flesh of man.
Came I forth from the body of my mother
Who has given me the flesh I call my own.

Though my body has come from my mother
It is made of the dust and clay of the earth.
I react to the world that surrounds me
With the flesh to which she's given birth.

On milk was I fed from my mother's bosom
And love and contentment I knew in her arms
Completely helpless was I born as an infant
My mother's love shielded me from all harms.

Warmth and attention she showered upon me
Of my needs and my comfort she was most aware
For everyone is born as a mere helpless infant
Everyone needs motherly love, help and care.

Fearful she is for me and proud of my efforts
Her love and protection are constantly there
Pain and suffering she allays with her presence
Her encouraging voice removes all my despair.

When I am hurt or in pain she suffers with me
And my failures in life she feels just as hard
When I cry out in triumph she rejoices with me
For my successes in life are a mother's reward.

Watchful and anxious she is for my welfare
For a mother's love has no limit or seams
Her love and affection she showers upon me
For my life is the base of my mother's dreams.

Father

My name is Adam, and I am man
My body is the body of man.
Born was I from an egg of a woman
And to my mother I owe my life.

But to my father also I owe my existence
The man who lived before me in time
For he is my model and mentor
Whose image and likeness I am.

Within his seed had I my beginnings
His cells and genes are the same as my own
His passion for life is the spark of my being
And this spark I now carry on as his son.

From this seed and egg have I been created
And their union of genes are all that I am
Of their blood and bone and fragile flesh
I am made in the likeness of man.

A life spark has been given me by my parents
To carry and pass into my children's hand
From them I received the baton of existence
To run my lap in the life race of man.

For they are my link to Adam
He was the first of all men
And all who have come to life after
Are naught but repetitions of him.

My name too, is Adam and I am man
And as man I enjoy the gift of life.
This gift I have received from my parents
To pass on to my children in turn.

As my parents struggled to overcome
The threats to my life and existence
So too, must I struggle to overcome
The threats to my children.

Growing Children

Little boys
Like making noise
Little girls
Like making murals.

Bigger boys
Like bigger toys
Bigger girls
Like pretty curls.

Grownup boys
Like grownup toys
Grown up girls
Like having pearls.

At each age
In the growing stage
Sexual differences
Cause personal preferences.

Children

My name is Adam, and I am man
Children I have to carry on my name.
My children are extensions of my life
And many are the dreams
I have had for them
That they may accomplish
What I have not.

Yet my dreams for my children cannot be
For they, too, are Adam and also man
And each must live a life
And dream dreams of their own.
For I cannot live their life for them
Better than they.

Many are the joys I have had
Guiding them to adulthood
And many are the hopes I have for them
And many are the fears I have felt
And many are the sorrows.
Many are the hours
I have spent in their company
And my spirit has soared
When they listened to my counsel.

From their infancy
I have watched them grow and develop
And many are the words of wisdom
I imparted to them
As I molded their intellects
And their spirits

Even as I supplied them
With food and shelter
And clothing for their bodies.
Yet many are the times
I have despaired
When they took not my counsel
And listened not to my words
But blundered into pitfalls
And learned the hard lessons of life
On their own.

I have mourned for them
Because I know that these lessons
Of life are necessary
And must be learned to become wise
And to understand.
With fear and trembling
I sent them out into the world
To struggle with hostile forces
And to meet the tests of living.

For I loved my children.
I showered them with care
And affection.
Many are the dreams
I dreamt for them
And many are the hopes
For their future and success in life.
I basked in the respect and love
They showered upon me.

I worked for them
And I fed and clothed them
And protected them from the cold.
I prayed for their welfare
And that they would find
Prosperity and peace of mind.
I fiercely desired to protect them
From evil and harm.

Two sons have I had
And the joy of seeing them
Grow into manhood.
I marveled at their strength
And their courage
And their development
Into independence.

But one son was filled with dissatisfaction
And rebelled against my counsel
And my way of life.
He followed not in my footsteps
But chose his own path
To make a place in the world.
He departed from that which I knew
And fearlessly went into the unknown.

I trembled and feared for him
For I know not what dangers
Lie in wait before him.
I know not how to counsel him
For I know not his future.

My other son listened to my counsel
And looked at my way of life
And found it good.
He took what I had built
And improved upon it and made it better.
In starting where I had ended
He built upon it
And exceeded what I had accomplished
Before him.

For his future I feared not
Because his footsteps
Are but extensions of my own.
I can foresee some of the hazards
And pitfalls before him.
I can counsel him how to avoid them
Even as I had avoided them.
Though there may be other hazards
And dangers that I cannot foresee,
They are not different in kind
And I fear them not for him.

Two daughters have I had
And the joy of seeing them
Grow into womanhood.
I marvel at their beauty
And their loving nature.

One daughter was rebellious
And would not listen to my counsel
Nor to the counsel of her mother.
She fiercely fought for her independence
And to find her own way in the world.

I feared for her
I trembled for her safety and happiness.
For I know not the pitfalls or hazards
That face her in a life I know not.
I reached out to hold her
But my arms could not bridge
The gap between us.

My other daughter listened to my words
And to the words of her mother
And found them good.
She followed in our footsteps
As if she would repeat our life
As her own.
I held her in my arms and cherished her
And delighted in her presence.

I pondered my sons and daughters
And the sons and daughters of others
And found it always to be thus.

Some there are
Who consider the works of their parents
And find them good and preserve them.
They build upon them
To improve still more that which is good.

And others there are
Who abandon the work of their fathers
That are not yet perfect.
These are the ones who would
Begin again to build a better world.

Some of the first succeed
In improving what they have received
From their fathers
While others fail.

And of the second some succeed
And many fail.
For difficult it is to make better
That which has withstood the test of time.
And difficult it is, indeed,
To make a better world.

Now,
In this ever-changing world
I no longer know
How to counsel my children
For they may succeed
And they may also fail
When they listen to my counsel.

Brotherhood

My name is Adam and I am man
My life is the life of man
For I exist as one cell among many
In the flesh and the body of man.

Then from inside my single cell
To other outside cells I see
Yet we are all linked together
In the whole of our humanity.

All alone I live in my single cell
And alone I must always remain
Even though I desire to go outside
And join with a like companion.

And though we number many
In mankind we are one
We live as separate entities
And each life is lived alone.

And many there were before me
And many yet await their birth
And many there are who live with me
And share my time here on earth.

We are akin in bone and fragile flesh
As we live our lives in togetherness
While we search for lasting harmony
In our travel to our destiny.

My name is Abel and I am man
And my spirit strives for the sky
To dance and sing with the angels
For all eternity when I die.

My name is Cain also and I am man
I suffer with a weakness of will
That is more akin to the animals
That snarl and quarrel and kill.

My name is Abraham and Jacob
And Joseph and Peter and Paul
And Nero and Napoleon and Hitler
For as men we are brothers in all.

My name is Magdaline and Mary
And Naomi and Martha and Anne
And Constance and Sarah and Catherine
For we are all together as man.

For these are our mothers and fathers
These are our brothers in man
We all share our life here together
According to God's predestined plan.

Sharing

My name is Adam and I am man
I live on earth with my fellow man.
We are all brothers
And we share the earth together.
We share the common inheritance
We received from our fathers.

We also share this time on earth
For what I do affects my brother
And what my brother does affects me.
We share our inheritance
In this place and time.

While we share this time
There is time enough for all.
For in sharing our time, we add to it
By sharing our work and our lives.

We also share the lives of those before us
Because we share the fruits of their labor.
We share the lives of our children
For they will receive the fruits of our work
As we have received from those who
Were before us in ages past.

With my brothers I share this place
What I do, I do for myself and my brother.
What he does, he does for himself and me.
For we share our existence
In this time and place.

But sometimes
There is not place enough for all.
So I cannot take the place I want
Because my brother is there.

Sometimes
There is not food enough for all
Then I cannot take all the food I want
For my brother also has need for food.

And that which I say and wish and do
May be to my brother's liking
By enriching his life to make it better.
And what my brother says and does
May be to my liking
By enriching my life to make it better.
Then I rejoice for his existence.

But sometimes I cannot do what I desire
For what I do affects my brother.
And some of the things that I do
May not be to his liking
And may make his life poorer
Because of what I have done.

And what my brother does
Has an affect on me.
For when he does
That which is not to my liking,
I am angered and saddened
Because my life is poorer
Because of what he has done.

Thus we share our existence
In this time and place
And our lives are not lived
For ourselves alone.

We must share our existence in life
And divide it evenly and fairly
And with justice and in peace.
For if I take more than my share
Or take it unfairly
Then I take from my brother
And my brother is angered.

Or if he takes more than his share
Or takes it unfairly
And with greed and excess
Then he takes from me what is mine
And I suffer and am saddened and
angered.

Thus my brother and I
Must learn to live our lives
In fairness and justice and love.
We must respect the needs of one another
And sacrifice our own desires
So we can share the fruits of the earth
and our labor in harmony and peace.

Section Five

Religious Poetry

Wheatfield

The panorama of wheat in the wheatfield
Is watched over by the eye of the grower.
He planted the seeds to grow the wheat
And watches it grow to maturity.
He waters it in due season
And sees each grain
In the mass of grains before him.

So, too, is Almighty God
Watching over each grain
In the wheatfield of humanity
As we grow to maturity.

Comes the harvest
The grower will winnow out the weeds
And the spoiled and shrunken grains
As the wheat flows by
To the granary.

Comes the day of judgment
So, too, will Almighty God
Examine each spirit
And winnow out the weeds
And the spoiled and shrunken souls
As the stream of mankind
Flows by
On the way to eternity.

Prayer

When I speak to the highest Power
Which I do several times each day
I speak first and then I listen
To hear what He has to say.

I ask Him for direction
How to live my life in time.
The answers that He gives me
Have helped to make my life sublime.

His counsel and His guidance
Has kept my heading true
And enabled my success in life
And in doing what I have to do.

He is with me in my sorrows
And when my life is full of woe
He is generous with His counsel
Pointing out which way to go.

I depend upon His power
To keep evil far away
I thank Him for assistance
And for good that comes my way.

You can whisper to the Power
About whatever you may care
You can be sure He'll listen
And will guide you everywhere.

The Lord's Request

If you've received the Father's blessing
And enjoy the life you're living
It does not seem too much to ask
To reconsider what you're giving.

The Lord would like a weekly visit
On one or the other of weekend days
To talk with Him for about an hour
To give Him thanks and sing His praise.

Then on your daily round of business
Take some time to spend in prayer
A total of ten minutes daily
Is time that everyone can spare.

And the Lord would like assistance
With a lot of work that you can do
For you're the one with hands to do it
When the Grace of God is helping you.

And when it comes to weekly giving
The Lord expects an ample sum
An hour's pay from every earner
Will help to make "His Kingdom Come."

A weekly hour spent in worship
An hour of service, pay and prayer
Is the way that leads to heaven
And is the means of getting there.

You Can Take It With You

Millionaires are often told
They must leave behind their gold
No matter what they do or try
They cannot keep it when they die.

So some will take the gold not spent
And build themselves a monument.
Others will leave their gold to heirs
Who'll spend it, soon as it is theirs.

Now if you have sought a way to keep it
My friend, you now can end your search
Because you can take your gold with you
Just by giving it to your church.

If you want to have some money
When you arrive at heaven's door,
The amount of gold you can take with you
Is the same amount you gave the poor.

And to those who live in mansions
Or for those who hold them dear
To have palatial home in heaven
Help give homes to the homeless here.

So heed my friend these words of wisdom
On your journey to the grave
The amount of gold you can take with you
Is not the amount you have but gave.

Shout With Joy on Christmas

REFRAIN
Shout with joy, clap your hands
And dance a little bit too!
Remember your Heavenly Father
Is watching over you!
Remember your Heavenly Father
Is watching over you!

1. An angel came to Mary
And said "You're the blessed one
Our Heavenly Father has chosen you
To be the mother of his Son."

2. When Mary went to Bethlehem
With Joseph as her spouse
There she gave birth to Jesus
In a stable not a house.

3. The angels told some shepherds
The Savior had been born
So they all went to see him
On that first Christmas morn.

4. Three wise men came from far away
To pay homage to the king
They had seen his glorious star
And had gold and gifts to bring.

5. Two thousand years have come and gone
Since the baby Jesus' birth
His name is known all o'er the world
And to everyone on earth

6. He came to teach us how to live
How to pray and how to love
He told us all we should believe
About God in heaven above.

7. So raise your eyes to heaven
And ask God for His grace
He will shower it down on you
And on the entire human race.

8. On Sundays when you go to church
To pray and sing his praise
He'll send you down his blessings
In many countless ways.

Street Bums

The courtyard was filthy dirty
And the bums were thick as fleas.
I held my breath as I passed by
So I wouldn't catch disease.

The beggars had their hands out
Wanting money to buy food
But the smell of liquor told me
They'd buy cheap wine if they could.

Another well-dressed gentleman
Was about to cross the court
So we started out together
To give each other moral support.

As we approached the far side
And gotten almost to the street
The other man stopped suddenly
To confront one cringing at his feet.

He looked at him intently
And then quickly in a flash
He took out his full billfold
And gave that poor bum all his cash.

Of course! I was surprised to see
How he took pity on that scum
And wondered why he passed the others
And been so generous with this bum.

So I asked him at the corner
When the light had turned to red.
He looked at me with shining eyes
And this is what he said:

"I know you think I'm crazy
But what you don't understand
The sight that really affected me
Was the NAIL HOLE in his hand."

Wanderlust

Eagles fly
Very high
Where they go?
I don't know!

If I could be
Just as free
Then I'd know
Where they go!

Though I try
I can't fly
So I'll never know
Where they go!

Letter From Heaven

Dear Friends,
I thought I'd write this letter
And to my earthbound friends confide
What happens to the soul of man
When the mortal man has died.

When I reached the pearly portal
There was a jam up at the gate
And I heard the voice of Peter
Say, "You newcomers have to wait."

It seems there was a sorting
Involving every single soul
It looked to me like half of them
Were being bypassed on the scroll.

The other half were beaming
When they finally learned their fate
They all were smiling broadly
As they skipped through the pearly gate.

It was chilly waiting up there
So I asked an angel for a coat
He rummaged around and found me
One not fit for man nor goat.

I said "What sleazy rag is this?"
And the angel said with glee
"My friend, that is the very coat
That you once proudly gave to me."

I took another look at him
And much to my surprise
He was a man I used to know
And now could hardly recognize.

He once had come to ask me
For help in a money matter
So I helped him out of a tough spot
And just threw in that old tatter.

He thanked me for my help again
It wasn't much I know
I didn't feel much better
'Cause you only reap what e'er you sow.

As I drew near the portal
I began to shiver somewhat more
Because it seemed to me the judging
Was getting tougher than before.

Then I noticed something else
About the angels flitting 'round
They looked like people I had known
When I was back on earthly ground.

And then it was my turn up front
For each angel to have his say
I saw that some were voting for me
While others voted nay!

My knees were all atremble
As I waited for the sign
And when the tally was complete
St. Peter said, "He's fine."

"But just give him a place in back
Because he didn't use his talents
He just gets in by the grace of God
And only then on balance."

I quick-stepped through the pearly gate
And heaved a grateful sigh
Because once inside those portals
The soul shall never die.

There is music, joy and laughter
And the thrill of victory
And even from my place in back
This is good enough for me.

If I had been more generous
With my money and my time
And given more help to others
I'd be further up the line

So to all you people there on earth
My suggestion is sincere
Be generous with your worldly goods
To get a better seat up here.

Forever yours,
Bill

Take Him Lord

Take him Lord!
Take my son,
Take him Lord!
If he's the one.

For I give him back to thee
As you gave him first to me.
Take him Lord!
For he belongs to thee.

Help him Lord!
Help him grow
Help him carry out thy will
And thy work.

For though I yearn to see
My son ever close to me
Take him Lord!
Because he belongs to thee.

I have had the joy of loving him
And helping him become a man.
Now I give him back to thee
According to your master plan.

Take him Lord!
For he belongs to thee.

Tithing

The Bible says that men should take
At least a tenth of what they make
And lay it at a poor man's feet
So the poor man's family can eat.

Some poor souls can't help their spot
And some may need your help a lot.
So overcome the vice of greed
And give some gold to those in need.

When you die and arrive at heaven
If you expect to get a welcome hand
Change your attitude toward giving
And heed the Bible's tithe command.

So when they pass the plate on Sunday
Give your fair portion to the Lord
He will in turn give it to the needy
And to godly men to spread his Word.

Section Six

Death and Dying

Dying

When I arrive at the time to die
I'll bid this world a last good-bye
For after death I expect to be
At the threshold of eternity!

And there beside the pearly gates
I'll meet Saint Peter as he waits
To sort the wheat from out the weeds
And weigh one's total words and deeds.

He holds the balance scales in hand
To weigh one's deeds with God's command
The good deeds done are brought to light
And balanced against the deeds of night.

If all the good I've done down here
Outweighs the bad in every year
I hope to wear the haloed crown
And not be prodded to go down.

For this will be the supreme test
To see if I have done my best
To live the life that I've been given
As my requisite to get to heaven.

Remember Me

Remember me, now that I'm gone
For fun and joy and laughter
Remember me for fortitude
In facing life hereafter.

Shed no tears for my demise
And give not in to sadness
For I have known without a doubt
My life was filled with gladness.

Mourn me not with sense of loss
Nor mourn my time of going
My life was full of joy and love
Which gave me pleasure knowing.

And wipe away those tears of pain
I'll hear no more of grieving
For I've completed my life's work
And now's the time for leaving.

So place my name in memory
And there please hold it fast
For calling up to reminisce
On fond memories of the past.

The Soul at Death

Just as the fetus in the maternal cage
Prepares itself for the following stage,
So, too, each person in his earthly days
Must prepare himself for the following
phase.

The unborn knows not what birth unfolds
So, too, man knows not what eternity holds.
As the unborn babe prepares for birth
So should all men prepare for death.

As the unborn stage will end in birth
So, too, will this life end in death.
What comes next as the unborn grows
Will far exceed what the fetus knows.

As the unborn's comprehension can expand
So will man's knowledge of the promised land.
For what comes next when the body dies
Will far exceed what we can surmise.

Oh Man! Prepare for the great transition
And get your soul in the right condition.
For when the time comes for you to die
You cannot come back for a second try.

Omega Time

As I grow older day by day
And my flesh grows weak and feeble
I ponder that which lies beyond
And what it holds for people.

For everyone should ponder
What lies beyond death's door
And if what and who we find there
Makes this life worth living for!

Because man is made of spirit
And is more than flesh and bone
He's more than just an animal
And earth is not his final home.

So should I fear the end of life?
And should I fear the judgment?
Should I fear the wrath of God
Or his final grand assessment?

But then I remember Jesus
And what he did and said
And the promises he made us
About the living and the dead.

So again I read the Good Book
And ponder words so wise
About the way to live my life
To insure my time in Paradise.

If I have lived my life in time
According to my talents
I should have no fear at all
Of my weighing in the balance.

If I have lived a proper life
According to God's prescription
The door to heaven should open wide
For me to gain admission.

So as I approach the end of life
And death comes ever near
I make my peace with God each day
Then I do not have to fear.

I can look forward to the time
When my name is called for testing
For there I'm sure that I will find
My name on heaven's listing!

Thus when I hear the trumpet
And know the calls for me
I'll gladly answer, "Here Sir"
And cross over to eternity.

I'll bid adieu to my earthly life
And leave all its cares behind
And cross the line to the other side
To join the saved souls of humankind.

So do not weep at my demise
And do not mourn my passing
For I'll have gone to a better place
Where Peace is everlasting.

So soar my soul away from here
To fly to heaven's portal
And leave this place in time and space
To join others now immortal.

For though I love those left behind
And know that they will mourn me
I rest assured in the course of time
Eventually they will join me.

For the spirit lives forever
While the flesh is in the grave
The person in the human
Is the part which shall be saved.

So live your life in goodness
And harm not your fellow man
But love and help your neighbor
To fulfill the Master's plan.

Section Seven

Humourous Poems

Dieting

One day my doctor told me that
I had gotten too darned fat
And if I didn't cut my eating back
I was heading for a heart attack.

He said I should stop eating sweets
And cut out eggs and fat and meats.
And as for drinking alcohol
I shouldn't drink any more at all.

I took the doctor at his word
And cut my calories by a third.
I lived on salad herbs and greens
Tofu, pasta types and beans.

I soon got healthy fit and trim.
Instead of fat I was quite slim.
But I liked the way I was before;
I know I sure enjoyed it more.

I know it's healthy to be gaunt
But this is not the life I want.
So I must decide which way I'll be
And indecision is killing me.

Because if I choose to live and eat
My life will then be short and sweet.
But if my taste buds I deny
I'll be very healthy when I die!

Jack Spratt

Jack Spratt was lean and trim
It was a Spratt tradition
He did some exercise everyday
And kept in good condition.

But Mrs. Spratt was much too fat
And no one could deny it
Yet every time she gained some weight
She put her husband on a diet.

Though Jack would holler loud and long
About the food that made him thinner.
He really didn't have much choice
Because she always made the dinner.

So one day Jack said "Let us talk
About our food and its priority."
But poor Jack lost the argument
Because her weight carried more
  authority.

Then Jack said "We have to vote
And our kitchen is the forum."
But Jack also lost his voting rights
Because by herself, she was a quorum.

Wine Is Good

Doctors say that wine is good
To clear one's arteries and blood.

And there really is no harm at all
In the moderate use of alcohol.

So buy a case of premium wine
And live it up for Auld Lang Syne,

Or go and get a cheaper jug
And drink it down by chug-a-lug.

For now we have a good excuse
To drink wine for its medicinal use.

We can take it for mental depression
Or as an aid to indigestion.

So sing with me the drinkers chorus,
"The stuff we drink is healthy for us."

Overweight

Too fat?
Deny it!
New diet?
So try it!
Can't fry it?
Decry it!
Oh! Be quiet!

Eagle Eye Dave

Young Eagle Eye Dave
A big Blackfoot brave
Came into town feeling frisky.
He got out of his car
Strolled into a bar
And ordered a shot of straight whiskey.

Now, the bartender knew
What the whiskey could do
So diluted the liquor with water.
When Dave tasted the stuff
He said, "I gotta get rough
So prepare yourself for some slaughter."

A cowboy in there
Got up from his chair
To subdue the bold Indian warrior.
When a man at the bar
Said, "The law makes it clear
To fight you must hire a lawyer."

Then Eagle Eye Dave
With a threatening rave
Said, "I will get Fights-with-Bear-Cubs.
He's been to some schools
And he knows all the rules
Then we'll come back and fight you with
war clubs."

The bartender looked
Just like he'd been spooked
And didn't want Indian trouble.
So he called the police
Who said, "This fighting must cease
Before this place is converted to rubble."

When the Indians returned
With the reputation they'd earned
The police were ready for action.
But when the Indians saw
They had to fight with the law
They agreed to a different transaction.

The bartender was blunt,
And said. "What do you want?"
Dave said. "I want a shot of straight liquor
And don't give me the guff
That I can't handle the stuff
Because I didn't come here to dicker."

The police said, "That's true
So here's what we'll do
We'll all smoke a peace pipe together,
Then the grass that we smoke
Will make us act like kinfolk
And be happy like birds of a feather."

The Vegetarian

Since I want to become
An octogenarian
My doctor told me
To become vegetarian.

Since I firmly believe
Change is futilitarian
I was doubtful I could
Become vegetarian.

So I went to a Guru
A known disciplinarian
Who promised to help me
Become vegetarian.

I was lucky that he
Was so authoritarian
Or I never could have
Become vegetarian.

He took over my life
As my regimentarian
In my quest to become
A complete vegetarian.

Now I'm a changed man
And no longer eat carrion
So I'm well on my way
To be an octogenarian.

Weeds

The bane of every gardener
Is the prolific growth of weeds
And he must pull those demons
Before they spread their seeds.

Or he will have a thicket
So rife with thistles and burdocks
That he can't see what he's planted
Except sunflowers and hollyhocks.

These weeds are always present
Because nature wants to show
How hard mortal man must labor
To get his garden plants to grow.

But nature does it easily
For the weeds themselves will spread
While man must struggle mightily
To earn his daily bread.

It says so in the Bible
That man must sweat his brow
And keeping weeds out of the garden
Is one way that says "Here's how."

Blue Plate Special

When I saw the busy diner
I thought I'd stop in on a hunch
The waitress recommended
The Blue Plate Special for my lunch.

The atmosphere was steamy
And full of tobacco smoke
The coffee was so atrocious
I wished I had ordered coke.

The waitress' hair was stringy
And kept falling in her eyes
The wad of gum she chewed on
Was at least a walnut's size.

Then when she brought my order
I saw that everything was fried,
She said "Now doesn't that look good?"
And I must admit I lied.

The food had run together
And everything was greasy
I suddenly lost my appetite
For my stomach had gotten queasy.

I asked the waitress for my bill
So I could flee that restaurant
But she said, "What's the matter,
Ain't the Special what you want?"

I told her I had changed my mind
And had to be on my way
But she called the cook to come on out
Because I couldn't leave that way.

The cook's apron was all dirty
And he hadn't bathed in weeks
The dirt beneath his fingernails
Matched the stubble on his cheeks.

In his hand he held a cleaver
There was fire in his eye
If someone didn't like his food
He demanded to know why.

Now I was in a quandry
I didn't know what to do
If I couldn't eat that sorry meal
It's the cook I'd answer to.

I glanced around to find escape
But every path seemed barred
The cook was glowering down at me
His eyes looked cold and hard.

I looked again at that plate lunch
And saw nothing but ptomaine
I knew if I tried to eat it
I would die in writhing pain.

When he raised the bloody cleaver
I knew why he meant to bring it
So I closed my eyes and grit my teeth
And said, "Go on and swing it!"

Terrier Triumph

The thunder was a'rumbling
And t'was raining very hard
When I heard a great commotion
Out there in my back yard.

I turned the back porch light on
And this is what I saw
It seems my dog and neighbor's cat
Were fighting tooth and claw.

The fur it was a'flying
The screeches curdled blood
The mews and barks were horrible
While they fought there in the mud.

The cat was finally beaten
And skedaddled up a tree
My dog gave one triumphant bark
Then came trotting back to me.

His coat was scratched and bloody
But he held his head up high
Although he was a sorry sight
He had victory in his eye.

I took him in and cleaned his wounds
And bestowed my master's pat
That dog was one proud animal
For he had bested that darned cat!

Young Cowboy

When people saw the young cowboy
from Buffalo Bend
They all thought he was starting
a new fashion trend.

When he paraded around
in the town's central square
They stopped what they were doing
and started to stare.

In his two gallon boots
and his ten gallon hat
He was a sight to behold
and worth staring at.

His new rhinestoned vest
and his black leather chaps
Completed his outfit
but left significant gaps.

The town marshal came
and after one startled glance
He said "Hey young cowboy,
where are your pants?"

The cowboy blushed crimson
and tried to cover his bottom
Then said to the marshal
"I just plumb forgot'em."

Fat Man's Lament

I know that I am too darn fat
I know my weight's appalling
I know it's 'cause I eat too much
For food is my downfalling.

Skinny people laugh at me
And encourage me to diet,
But if they had my metabolic rate
I'd like to see them try it.

I know that I should diet more
And I try with all my might,
But in the battle with my stomach
My tongue controls my appetite.

I'm tired of being overweight
Of breaking chairs and such,
I'm tired of seeing friends repulsed
Because I weigh too much!

I know my weight's a problem
I know I'm much too stout
For within this flesh a skinny soul
Is trying desperately to get out.

Retirement

On the day of my retirement
When my workdays were all past
I raised my eyes to heaven
"Thank God I'm free at last."

Now in these precious golden years
I can do as I desire
My time is controlled by me alone
There is no boss man higher.

There are no hectic mornings
When I'm racing with the clock
No more nerve wracking traffic jams
That exist on every block.

There are no frantic Saturdays
With a million things to do
And no more long hours of overtime
Until an important job is through.

Now, if there is a pressing chore
I trust the task will keep
Until some time tomorrow
Because I'm going back to sleep!

Conversational Tennis

Some conversations that I watch
Are often like a tennis match.
The words are batted back and forth
But the entire talk is seldom worth
The time it takes to listen to
The things they say but seldom do.

And when the thought is talked to death
The talkers stop to catch their breath
Then take up where they were before
And talk and talk and talk some more.
Although tennis is a finite endeavor
Some people seem to talk forever.

Flying Saucers

When saucers come from outer space
They can upset the populace.
But I would like to meet these men
And learn about their stratagem
For travel through the universe
And other subjects quite diverse.

But they seem to evade contact
Not knowing how we will react!
Perhaps they fear us human types
And the guns we use to settle gripes.
It gives me pause to question why
But little wonder, so do I!

Grandchildren

We're off to see the grandkids
Hurrah! Hurrah! Hurray!
We want to see how much they've grown
Since last we went their way.

We want to hold them in our arms
And squeeze the little dears
'Cause we've missed the little darlings
And want to share their childhood years.

We love the little rascals
And can't wait to see their smiles
And hear their shouts of welcome
After driving all those miles.

We know they'll jump with happiness
And clap their hands with glee
Because grandparents are so special
That they're always good to see.

Our spirits are uplifted
When we see happiness in their eyes
We know they enjoy our visits
And what we bring as a surprise.

For it surely is delightful
To visit the little elves
So mother dear and daddy
Can have a night out by themselves.

We take over for an evening
So Mom and Dad can get away
To spend a quiet evening
In an adult kind of way.

We play the children's games with them
And sing the children songs
Because our visit's like a party
Where every one belongs.

They wear us out with playing
Until we're tired and want to stop
But they keep us there by saying
They want to play until they drop.

We read the same old stories
That we have read to them before
And though we're tired of reading
They always want us to read some more.

It's finally time for dinner
And after we've said grace
The food that started on the plate
Winds up on every little face.

The milk is spilt all over
And the spaghetti's on the floor
They smear the food both high and low
And then they cry for more.

They blow bubbles in the milk glass
And dribble it down their chin
The mess is unbelievable
And you can't hear above the din.

You clean up all the mess again
And wash their hands and faces
Pick up the food from off the floor
So it's safe to leave their places.

Then pretty soon its time for baths
And Oh! what a doleful pout
But once you get them in the tub
You can hardly get them out.

To get them into their pajamas
You have to make it like a game
Then their prayers for Gram and Grampa
Make you mighty glad you came.

Of Course! You have to read to them
And help them count their sheep
They certainly look like angels
When they are finally fast asleep.

Then grandmama and grandpa
At last can hit the hay
Because by now they are exhausted
For it has been a long long day.

And then along about two A.M.
You hear a little cry
So you jump up in a hurry
To go and see the reason why.

The little one is wet again
And is that a croupy cough?
Oh no! He's simply gotten chilly
Because he kicked the covers off!

Then early in the morning
You hear a little sleepy head
He's gotten up and found you
And wants to come inside your bed.

You snuggle up and hold him
Close and warm inside your arms
As if you'd like to keep him
Ever safe from cold and harms.

When the wriggle gets excessive
You know its time to rise
So you struggle to get out of bed
And rub the sleep out of your eyes.

Of course! the kids are wide awake
For its time to start the day
Because when Grampa's up and ready
They have more games they want to play.

And then its time for breakfast
And all the spills and smears begin
While you longingly look toward the door
Until its time to leave again.

Good-byes are always painful
While you linger at the door
And give each child a final hug
And then say good-bye some more.

And as the car pulls from the curb
You wave a last good-bye
Then resolutely turn your head
And heave a grateful sigh.

Its nice to see the grandkids
Hurrah! Hurrah! Hurray!
For though you do enjoy the visit
Boy! Its nice to drive away!

Traffic Ticket

When you're stopped for erratic driving
And can't think of a good excuse
The officer won't take your word
That you were drinking orange juice!

Black Bart PO8

Folks say I am a robber
That I make my money stealing
But if I were a banker
They would just call it dealing!

Along a lonely stretch of road
I hide within the trees
Then stop the stage when it comes by
By saying "If you please."

I hold the stage at gunpoint
And say, "Throw down the box."
The reason they can't catch me
I'm as clever as a fox.

I use an empty flour sack
To hide my face and hair
So no one can recognize me
And claim that I was there!

I only stop the stages
That belong to Wells and Fargo
So I can make withdrawal
Of the money in the cargo.

I do not rob the passengers,
Harm the driver or his horses.
I get more money this a'way
Than I can from other sources.

Some day I will be captured
For robbing public stages
Then surely they will put me
In one of San Quentin's cages.

But until that sad occurence
My life is filled with pleasure
I buy nice things and pay my bills
By using Wells Fargo's treasure!

Work Ethic

Unless every clerk
Get down to work
The big bad boss
Will get very cross!

Ready Cash

When your bank account it empty
And your credit's over drawn
You can't raise extra money
Putting your children into pawn!

Small Talk

When men and women meet together
Some talk sense while others blather.

Wise people know the spoken word
Can often be somewhat absurd.

If you must talk at least make sense
So those who hear don't have to wince.

Or better yet don't talk at all
If your tongue is loose'd by alcohol.

SECTION EIGHT

Poetry and Writing

Words, Words, Words

Words are thoughts that resonate
And are used by folks to communicate.
They can be written, spoke or sung
And used by anyone with tongue.

These words are what all authors use
And they have lots from which to choose.
The dictionary is the source
Which they use quite a bit. Of course!

We authors can use various tricks
To build a wall with words like bricks,
We pick and choose and make them fit
Into our writing bit by bit.

You start with paper clean and white,
Set yourself down and start to write,
Then choose your words with utmost care
Though you can find them everywhere.

Think it up
Write it down.

For verse
Be terse.

But for a novel
Use a shovel!

Poetic Expression

When poets start to ponder
Perceptions of the day
Their minds begin reflecting
On what they have to say.

They start with some ideas
Then search for a connection
To tie the thoughts together
By careful introspection.

Creative thoughts are in the mind
And should be gotten out
Then written down in poetic form
For other minds to think about.

So when you read a poem
Let your imagination bound
And try to feel the poet's mood
In the poetic world of sound.

?

Verse is nerse
But so's prose.

Poets Ponder

Poets ponder
Words of wonder
Thoughts to give an inward thrill
Poetic praises
Fertile phrases
Make the heart beat faster still.

Desire driving
Constant striving
Groping for the perfect word
Introspecting
Then selecting
So that special sound is heard.

Planning pleasures
Matching measures
Give the poem a pleasing sheen
Words selected
Then connected
So the beauty can be seen.

Poems inspire
Spirits higher
When you contemplate the whole
Fellow feeling
Self revealing
Exhilarate the hearer's soul!

Memorable Poetry

Some of my poems are pretty good
And some are simply rotten
So some should be remembered
And others just forgotten.

For those that are remembered
I'm sure I will gain fame
But those that are forgotten
Are writ' by "what's his name?'

My poetry has the purpose
To lift one's spirits higher
But if it does the opposite
Consign it to the fire!

Thus when you read my poetry
Store some in memory's cache
Remember those that appeal to you
And throw the others in the trash!

Poetic Trends

It used to be that poetry
Had form and rhyme and rhythm
And ears that heard the spoken word
Knew that sense was carried with 'em.

But now the trend seems to portend
That rhyme is not important
The rhythm too, you can eschew
And form is too discordant.

So now we see in poetry
Sense replaced by sheer abstraction
And what is left is quite bereft
Of any mental interaction.

Oh! Would this trend come to an end
So form would be admired
Then rhythm and rhyme could reign sublime
And sense be once more required!

Rabbit

Sees me
Flees me

Snake in the Grass

See it
Flee it

Writing Good Poetry

There are some people who tend to repeat
all the time
That poetry does not have to use rhythm
and rhyme
And poetry does not have to have a form
like before
And it does not even have to make sense
anymore.

These people use what is laughingly known
as free verse
But the stuff that they write cannot be written
much worse
If readers cannot tell what the poet is
trying to say
They may think that all poetry has to be
written this way.

I would like to show these people again
one more time
Good poetry should be written
in rhythm and rhyme.
And this good poetry is smooth and has
things to say
So that some day all good poetry will
be written this way.

Fledgling Poet

(Following the tune of Yankee Doodle Dandy)

CHORUS
Fledgling poets keep it up
Keep your Thesaurus handy
Mind the meter and the feet
And use your rhyming grandly.

1. Fledgling poets try their best
So they won't be called phony
They write it down then tear it up
And don't make any money.

2. They hope one day to be well known
For poems they have written
Because it is with poetry
Their senses have been smitten.

3. They once read a pretty poem
And thought it was exciting
If they can write some just as good
They'll make their living writing.

4. They think of words that sound quite good
When they tell it to the mirror
Then parse and prune it o'er and o'er
To make the meaning clearer.

Section Nine

Patriotic Poems

The Constitution

It is just a piece of parchment
With the words of man's intent
To create a constitution
For the form of government.

It says that "We the people"
Have united in a cause
To ordain an ideal system
To enact the nation's laws.

The words reflect the wisdom
Of the founders' noble thoughts
That people of all backgrounds
Have common rights and common lots.

They have a common welfare
And will defend a common ground.
They want a life that's tranquil
For happiness to be found.

There are no kings or princes
Because the people are supreme
And everyone is equal
In the struggle for the dream.

The rule shall be divided
Among three equal spheres
With many checks and balances
To assure that everyone adheres.

It requires free elections
And provides for all to choose
Which ones will be the leaders
To decide the laws to use.

It sets up a noble office
For the chief executive
Who shall be the chief enforcer
Of the way that we shall live.

The laws will be interpreted
To conform to its command
That pronouncements of the highest court
Shall be supreme throughout the land.

It provides two august chambers
To debate the pro and con
Of how much to raise in taxes
And what to spend the money on.

One house shall be a Senate
That shall deliberate
What laws are best for people
That shall be used in every state.

One house shall have as members
The best elected candidates
To represent the numbers
Of the people in their states.

The two elected houses
Shall enact the nation's laws
And will advise the President
On how to mend the nation's flaws.

A Bill of Rights was added
To guarantee to you and me
The blessings of the freedom
Our forefathers could foresee.

Then they allowed amendments
To be added to the ten
To establish new dimensions
When the people wanted them.

These precious words on parchment
Have withstood the test of time
And if all nations would adopt them
The whole world would be sublime.

So revere this noble parchment
And the words recorded there
It's the world's best hope for justice
And for freedom everywhere.

The American Flag

Oh! Look up and see
That flag in the sky
It's America's symbol
That's flying so high.

It flies over a nation
With laws that are good
For the promotion of freedom
Peace and brotherhood.

We've come from all over
To this melting pot
Where all people are equal
In this nation we've got.

Our skins are all colors
Our creeds not the same
But we all share in having
That great American name.

Our heritage is different
Yet united we stand
As one mighty nation
In a very proud land.

We cherish its ideals
We subscribe to its themes
For this American nation
Is the land of our dreams.

So raise up these colors
For all people to see
Because America's promise
Is that all must be free.

Thus when any one living
For freedom shall cry
That's when this symbol
Of freedom shall fly.

Then free men shall rally
And answer the call
For the enslavement of one
Is a threat to us all.

All heroes shall muster
And prepare for a war
To fight for men's freedom
As did our fathers before.

So fight you brave soldiers
This cause must not fail
For the rule of the tyrant
Shall never prevail.

For hope is a watchword
And In God is our Trust
When we fight as a nation
For laws that are just.

So raise high this banner
With its folds all unfurled
As a symbol of justice
All over the world.

And cheer when you see it
As proudly we sing
Of the American nation
Where people are king.

Then cherish this banner
*And long may it wave
*O'er the land of the free
*And the home of the brave.

*From the Star Spangled Banner
by Francis Scott Key

The Eagle

Fly high
Soar more
Fish snatch
Great catch!

Flying Flag

When you see our flag a'flying
And a'rippling in the breeze
You may think that personal freedom
Means doing what you please.

When you see the flag a'flying
And a'flapping in the air
Remember that rights of others
Are paramount everywhere.

When you see the flag is hoisted
And is hanging on its pole
You know that all Americans
Demand justice as our goal.

For if a tyrant ever threatens
To cause our country harms
We shall rally 'round this banner
And unite to take up arms.

We shall fight to maintain freedom
We shall fight with plane and gun
We shall mount a mighty effort
To win the fight which must be won.

Then when we've won the victory
And our lives again secure
We shall rally 'round our standard
And give our flag a mighty cheer.

When you see the stars and striping
Flying high up in the sky
You can tell this mighty nation
Has resolved to never die.

For the flag you see a'flying
Stands for justice without fear
Because it's the symbol of our nation
And the people living here.

So when you see the flag a'flying
Thank your God on bended knee
That you're living in a nation
Where everyone is free.

Scientists Say

Scientists say that humans
Are the animal's aristocrat
But I don't know any animals
That would agree with that.

The Beacon of Freedom

To light the dark corners
All over the earth
A symbol is needed
To aid freedom's birth.

This symbol of freedom
Shall shine with a beam
Of man's burning desire
For the liberty dream.

On a magnificent tower
This beacon shall rise
And like man's aspirations
Point to limitless skies.

At the birthplace of Nations
United it stands
As symbolic of freedom
For all peoples and lands.

So when any man living
For freedom shall yearn
That's when the beacon
Of freedom must burn

Then ignite the beacon
And brighten its flame
To shine for the oppressed
In Freedom's sweet name.

Then all heroes shall muster
And flock to the cause
To fight for man's freedom
Brotherhood and just laws.

For God is your standard
And Hope is your right
His Power shall protect you
When for freedom you fight.

So let's build this great beacon
For all people to see
As man's determination
That all must be free.

Alert for Liberty

Oh! See the brave conquering hero
Who marches with banners unfurled,
He claims he has all the programs
To right all the wrongs in the world.

Where did he get all the knowledge
Of the future so well understood
That he can claim to know what is best
And how to change the bad into good.

Trust not the hypocritical dictator
Whose compassion is expressed with a tear
Who decries the plight of the needy
And tells them all what they wish to hear.

For anyone who can correct all injustice
Has every right to be proud
But that which is good for the tyrant
Is seldom the same for the crowd.

For does the tyrant really want fairness?
Will he really do all that he should
To overcome all the injustice
And replace all the bad with the good?

Beware that all powerful tyrant
Who seeks progress without any delay
For the easiest means to achieve it
Is just to kill everyone in the way.

For the wrath of the self-righteous tyrant
Is fearful to see and behold
For the tyrant's lust for more power
Is like the miser's greed for more gold.

Beware the proud leader with power
Because his lust can quickly deprave
*And the evil he does will live after
While the good is interred in his grave.

So when you hear the cadence of soldiers
And their hobnailed boots in the street
Look quickly to see if your freedom
Has been ground in the dust at their feet.

Look quickly to see if religion
Can be practiced and left unopposed
And look quickly to see if the churches
And any synagogues have recently closed.

Then see if your morning newspaper
Can print all the news in the land
And see if the right to speak freely
Or the right to read books has been
banned.

And have you heard any rumors
Of torture and death in the jail?
And have any students been missing
Or have the courts refused to grant bail?

And can you still freely assemble?
Can you talk freely with friends?
For acting together in concert
Is a right on which freedom depends.

For freedom to read, speak and assemble
And to pray to your personal God
Are the first things the tyrant must banish
For his armies to rule with the rod.

~ ~ ~

These rights are essential
For the small and the great
To guarantee justice
In the all-powerful state.

For justice is periled
And fairness unknown
When a tyrant's in power
And liberty has flown.

For freedom is fleeting
And death's always at hand
When the whim of the tyrant
Is the law of the land.

So fight against tyrants
Whatever the cost
For it's too late for precaution
When your liberty is lost.

*After Shakespeare, Julius Caeser, Act III

Hordes

Hordes of humanity
Avoiding calamity
And hoping for amity
Come to the good old US of A.

They come voluntarily
To make money primarily
Then stay necessarily
Here in the good old US of A.

They stay in localities
With their own nationalities
Where they enjoy commonalties
Here in the good old US of A.

Some see it clearly
They must live austerely
Or they'll suffer severely
Here in the good old US of A.

But those with ambition
And a work disposition
Can improve their condition
Here in the good old US of A.

Section Ten

Warfare

Prologue to War

There comes a time in every nation
When its citizens must gird for war
Because liberty and justice
Are principles worth fighting for.

As all history has shown us
When in terms of the common good
Equal justice is the watchword
Which brings peace and brotherhood.

And when slavery is considered
Free men have always understood
That the bill for people's freedom
Must be paid in hero's blood.

For when a tyrant usurps power
People's wishes are ignored
And the urge for personal freedom
Is then thwarted by the sword.

For the tyrant never rests secure
And must rule with gun in hand
So the lives of all are threatened
And justice' fled from out the land.

You must resist the ruthless despot
And do not join his lawless throng
For there always is injustice
When the king is in the wrong.

And do not listen to his rhetoric
As he struts throughout the land
Because the promises of despots
Are as written on the sand.

But mankind's peaceful aspirations
Cannot be forever kept at bay
Because the mighty tides of justice
Shall wash the tyrant's words away.

Appeasement

And then there are appeasers
Who should hang their heads in shame
For they claim to stand for justice
But will not fight in justice's name

They enjoy the fruits of freedom
And can say what e'er they will
But they claim to be exempted
From their share of freedom's bill.

Though they claim a lofty purpose
That they stand on moral ground,
Yet the reality of injustice
Makes their logic quite unsound.

So they demonstrate with clamor
And enjoy what freedom yields
Yet they riot and cause disorder
And ignore all sane appeals.

So castigate these wretches
Who'd surrender freedom without fight
For they'd tolerate injustice
Out of fear of the tyrant's might.

Preconditions for War

When people groan with frustration
And grovel under the boot of the king
There is no course save rebellion
And the peace that justice can bring.

When the people cry out for salvation
But justice's scales are hanging askew
People's rights have been abrogated
And the many are abused by the few.

When the will of the people is stymied
With justice nowhere to be found
Then all hope and man's aspirations
Are thwarted and stomped in the ground.

Prepare then to fight for your freedom
So liberty and justice endure
Because happiness only can flourish
When everyone's life is secure.

To achieve this peaceful condition
The tyrant must be overthrown
For the anguish and bloodshed of warfare
Is the result of justice unknown.

When all the words have been spoken
But the tyrant's ears seem to be deaf
Then the time for talking is over
And nothing but fighting is left.

Waging War

So breakout the rifles and ammo
And issue arms to all men in the ranks
Then load up the bombers with bomlets
And service and arm all of the tanks.

When injustice is no longer accepted
And the people have risen in wrath
The war and the bloodshed that follow
Is the result of the tyrant's wrong path.

When you hear the drone of the bombers
And the ratatatat of the gun
The first screams of anguish will signal
That the war for relief has begun.

When the entire earth is atremble
Midst exploding bomb bursts and flame
Soldiers will cower in foxholes
And know that war is hell's other name.

For there in the midst of destruction
In the blast of bomb burst and shell
In the midst of the dying and bloodshed
No one can ever deny war is hell.

You can hear the screams of the children
When they see that their mothers have died
And what is seen all around is destruction
With no secure place they can hide.

When ear drums are shattered by shell bursts
And eyes are sated with blood and with gore
Midst the terror and horror of battle
Know you then that you are at war.

In the noise and confusion and terror
All are killed by shell bursts and flame
For in war there are no exemptions
And everyone is killed just the same.

When entire cities are flattened
And homes destroyed by fire and bomb
The rubble of man's peaceful endeavors
Can be interred with him in his tomb.

The horror and bloodshed of warfare
Is the price the survivors must know
For justice and freedom to flourish
To permit the human spirit to grow.

Only after the tyrant is ousted
With the people once more in command
Can the sounds of the battle grow silent
And peace return once again to the land.

When the noise of the battle is over
And the sound of the cannon is still
The innocent laughter of children
Can be heard once again on the hill.

Then soldiers can lay down their rifles
And scrap all the weapons of war
To live once again as civilians
And continue their lives as before.

Aftermath of War

So cheer the brave men returning from battle
For they have faced the horror and terror of war
They have been close to deadly destruction
And have been witness to death, carnage and gore.

They've had to face death in many a battle
When reason and sanity were replaced by fear
Their friends all around had fallen in combat
And sudden violent death was always too near.

Be grateful for the safe return of the heroes
After they have endured deprivation and pain
Be grateful they have survived in the battles
And pray they may never wage warfare again.

Remember the warriors who were wounded in warfare
And have great compassion for the pain that they bear
For wounds they've suffered have scars that are lasting
And many will always need treatment and care.

Remember the many with minds that are mangled
Whose mental well-being has been shocked by the shell
Their dreams are affected by nightmares and demons
And their lucid memories are one living hell.

And pray for the soldiers who died in the battle
And mourn for the sailors who were buried at sea
Their young lives were given for what they believed in
Their young lives were given for you and for me.

And pray for the many who are missing in action
And comfort the loved ones who still haven't heard
If the loved who are missing are dead or still living
And pray for them most when they get final word.

Pray for the soldiers who are prisoners of warfare
And praise them for valor for the pain they've endured
Be thankful for those who survive the grim ordeal
And pray for the ones that succumbed when injured.

Pray for the people who fled from the battle
And lost their possessions to bombing and flame
When they return to their homes in the rubble
Pray that they can rebuild, though it's never the same.

Pity the people who have fled from their homeland
And due to circumstances can never return
For in foreign lands they ever must wander
While new language and customs they desperately learn.

Pray for the survivors who lost all their family
So now have no kindred to claim as their own
For all those around them are no one but strangers
And all of their memories are remembered alone.

Weep for the widow who lost all her children
And now has no offspring to claim as an heir
She has lost all her reason to continue on living
And now lives her life in dark hopeless despair.

Aye! Weep for the women who are widowed by warfare
The embrace of their husbands can no longer comfort
And weep for the children, now fatherless orphans
What will they miss always, is his love and support.

Pray for all those who are no longer living
And pray for the living who must carry on
Remember that warfare means destruction and killing
So that everything cherished is demolished and
gone.

Winning the Peace

In peace we can live in civil tranquility
If laws are enacted that are balanced and fair
All can live in peace and quiet contentment
If justice is universal and all have a share.

For peace and domestic tranquility
Will bloom when the tyrant is gone
And each person can do as he wishes
Because of freedom the heroes have won.

For after the tyrant is vanquished
The killing and destruction can cease
Then the victor can boast of his triumph
And can dictate the terms of the peace.

But the peace can never be final
If resentment and anger remain
For injustice and harsh retribution
Will cause fighting and bloodshed again.

So the victor must exercise mercy
And grant amnesty to those who have lost
For the ignominy of being defeated
Is a significant part of the cost.

But if the victor shows his compassion
And is just and fair with his ends
The peace that ensues will be lasting
When the two warring groups become
friends.

For true peace among men is elusive
And can quickly dissolve into strife
If the victor is overly vengeful
And tries to punish the losers for life.

For peace to be found among peoples
Requires justice and freedom for all.
Then trade and commerce can flourish
So that peace is a blessing for all.

Entreaty

Perhaps sometime in the future
It will be everywhere understood
That warfare is never the answer
And seldom does anyone good.

And some time out there in the future
A worldwide way must be found
To deter and prevent any aggression
So peace can be kept safe and sound.

And perhaps in the progress of mankind
Someone will develop technique
To resolve the conflicts between peoples
So warfare will be considered antique.

When peace is made among peoples
Man's earthbound spirit can soar
And while there may always be conflicts
There need not always be war.

For if war can be made obsolescent
The woeful wastage of warfare can cease
When mankind learns to live fairly together
The whole world can enjoy genuine peace.

Section Eleven

Political Poems

Politicians

There is a ritual in this nation
That requires citizen participation
For we have to choose the ones to give
The power to tell us how to live.

We have to choose one from a few
Who want to control the things we do.
Yet after all is done and said
The choice we have is limited.

Because each candidate always tries
To convince us with a bunch of lies
And by making promises he can't keep
He treats us voters just like sheep.

These politicians make me sick
With their words so smooth and slick
They say invest instead of spend
But it means the same thing in the end.

Or they say they want a user's fee
But it sounds like a tax to me
And enhanced revenue is how its phrased
To hide the fact that a tax is raised.

For to represent the people right
They should hold the purse strings tight
And not pass laws that waste the tax
That they've extracted from our backs.

Remember this when you vote my friend,
The power to tax is the power to spend.
And examine the way your money's spent
After it's been taken by the government.

Consider the way the government's run
When you vote for good that can be done
For the actual fact that must be faced
That government spending is mostly waste.

When things are bad, we should remember
That comes the day in the next November
We can exercise our voting might
By electing ones to set things right.

For in this vast and fruitful land
There are many other ones who can
Run for office without a doubt
So we can throw the incumbents out.

But be careful what you vote to get
For worse things could still happen yet
And you're the ones who have to pay
If those big spenders have their way.

And there is another perplexing note
When you decide to cast your vote,
And that's if no one seems first rate
How do you select your candidate?

You should vote for one you trust
But what if they all fill you with disgust?
What do you do if you must choose
Because others will if you refuse?

You can choose what seems the lesser evil
Or which one will cause the less upheaval.
And then hope that the one elected
Will turnout better than expected.

For elections are a sacred trust
That our forefathers placed in us.
We all must vote and thus insure
That our great nation will endure.

Opinion

A difference of opinion
Can lead to heated words
Especially when both parties
Are practiced lyrebirds!

Political Speeches

When politicians start to speak
I find it's time for me to seek
A quiet place to think about
What electioneering is all about.

When I hear what they have to say
It nearly ruins my whole day
For though it sounds quite good you see
I know its just hyperbole.

I listen to their point of view
And analyze what they say they'll do.
While some words have majestic sweep
Most are just promises they won't keep.

The words come out so thick and fast
I seldom hear such loud bombast.
If I listen close, my ears recoil
From such a flood of barnyard soil.

I wish I had a truth machine
So I'd know precisely what they mean.
Though if I could believe their scam
I'd be more disgusted than I am.

The Politician's Curse

There must be a curse
That makes everything worse
Regardless of previous conditions
For if a curse there is such
It's exposed by the touch
Of almost all of today's politicians.

When they pass the laws
To correct all the cause
Of a problem as they can perceive it
They don't vote as they should
When they try to do good
Since the laws always seem to aggrieve it.

Though they try to relieve it
They seldom achieve it
Since politicians seem to use a reverser
Because when they get involved
The problems not solved
Their laws make conditions much worser.

For the truth to be told
When there's a right to uphold
Though politicians always try to secure it
After thousands of exceptions
And erroneous conceptions
Their laws do not always ensure it!

The Singer And The Song

Frequently in every nation
Where democracy is strong
The citizens must choose someone
To be the leader of the throng.

There are usually several candidates
And each can speak with silver tongue
But they're not believed by many
Except for idiots and the young.

They make a lot of promises
As the campaign rolls along
With their self-applauding voices
Exalting the singer and his song.

Their promises are rosy
For more jobs and healthful days
And not to worry about the cost
Because its the government that pays.

They say they'll cut your taxes
Because they are not justified
And have millionaires pay all the bills
Because the candidate is on your side.

They say they'll lock up criminals
Then throw away the key
They'll remove the cause of all the crime
And stop the police brutality.

The voters have heard all this before
Amid the rhetoric loud and long
For they know that life can never be
As claimed by the singer and his song.

So they vote with trepidation
Since they know the siren's wrong
Although they always get a singer
They very seldom get his song.

Unexpected Choice

When the bargirl met the sailor
She invited him to her bed
He just said, "No. But thanks a lot
I'm going to church instead!"

Candidate's Promises

Some politicians always seem to be
A bunch of lying crooks to you and me.
The things they say when they are on the stump
Are promises that they just simply dump.
The voter's wishes they just plain ignore
And pass bad laws just like they did before.
What can we people as plain voters do
To get our electees to follow through
And do the things that they so boldly said
That they would do if they controlled the Fed.
There ought to be a way to force them to
And vote the way they said that they would do.
  I think the law should let us kick behinds
  Of electees who said they've changed their minds.

Government Spending

I sometimes wonder how my money's spent
When it's been taken by the government.
I wonder if the need for citizens
Is nothing more than as a source of funds.
So government can go it's spending way
Without a thought of those who have to pay.
And when it comes to passing special laws
The elected ones all seem to have a cause
That they promote and then make shady deals
For those back home to repay cash appeals.
I wonder where their honesty has gone
And wonder what they base their judgment on.
  And how their consciences can stand the strain
  To run and make such promises again.

Old King Canute

Old King Canute was known as a brute
And King Canute was tough
He ran his realm with an iron hand
Until his subjects hollered, "Enough."

Queen Canutti was known as a beauty
And Queen Canutti was fair
She spent her days in a beauty salon
By fussing all day with her hair.

Princess Patricia was pretty
And Princess Patricia was proud
She stared at all with an imperious glare
Until everyone present had bowed.

The Prince of the kingdom was nutty
For the Prince of the kingdom was mad
When he heard the subjects planned to rebel
He danced for joy and was glad.

The kingdom seethed with rebellion
Because the king raised the taxes so high
And some of the subjects were starving
While many were just getting by.

So they chased the king out of the country
And took over the kingdom by force
Then followed a new fearless leader
Because he was the one on the white horse.

When the general took over the country
His word became the law of the land
But people paid the price with their freedom
And had to obey his autocratic command.

Then once again the people were angry
Because the general was as bad as the king
For replacing kings with dictators, shows
Changing tyrants does not change a thing.

This time they vowed there'd be changes
And the people resorted to war,
They fought off the dictator's soldiers
So that justice could reign evermore.

They voted to establish new leaders
To govern the nation with laws
With a constitution adopted for guidance
To find and correct all the flaws.

Now the citizens are mostly contented
They vote what they want to achieve
And all the disgruntled others
Must conform to the law – or leave.

Ode To The New President

Bill Clinton's gone to Washington
For his first inauguration
He's gone to take command of things
As proud leader of our nation.

For one day he will hear the cheers
And receive the adulation
But then he must get down to work
With stern determination.

The problems that are facing him
Will cause much consternation,
Solutions will be hard to find
And result in tribulation

The deficit is looming large
But there can't be more taxation
He must find ways to cut the cost
Though it causes aggravation.

The people's health is not so good
And some suffer deprivation
So people are expecting him
To provide alleviation.

Some citizens cannot find jobs
In their chosen occupations
So they all look to Washington
To fulfill their expectations.

The Congress has assembled there
To pass the legislation
And change the cause of all the woes
To improve the situation.

The people anxiously await
With eager anticipation
For him to do what he promised to
In return for their donation.

Good Luck! Bill, and so help you God
With your administration
If you can perform miracles
You'll earn our admiration!

Sarcasm

Sarcastic remarks
Especially in writing
Can hurt both of the parties
Just like in cock-fighting.

Presidential Promises

You may like President Clinton
But you can't trust his word
He's broken more promises
Than you've ever heard.

He said he'd make tax cuts
But he raised them instead
He said "I know what I promised
But I didn't mean what I said."

"The statements I ran on
Are not quite what I meant
And I've since changed my mind
Now that I'm President."

"The problems are larger
Than I ever thought
And good liberal solutions
Are nowhere to be bought."

So resist the temptation
To take him at his word
For the promises he made us
Are absolutely absurd.

Clinton Tax Cut/Hikes

Sing a song of tax cuts
Soak it to the rich
Once you're safe in office
You can make a switch!

Change your mind on tax cuts
Soak the voters all
Give your friends exemptions
All it takes is gall!

Place the blame on Congress
Tell the Press to hush
Place the blame on Reagan
Or better yet George Bush!

Sing a song for tax hikes
You want to spend the dough
To hell with the huge deficit
We'll just let it grow.

Claim you need to spend more
To help the economy
And pay off special interests
And liberal bourgeoisie!

You have to raise the taxes
Or you're not a Democrat
Because raising people's taxes
Is where that Party's at!

Sing a song of tax hikes
Claim the nation has a need
For its the basic principle
In the Democrat Party creed!

Clinton's Speeches

President Clinton tells untruths
And outrageous lies
He speaks so damn engagingly
He can fool us with his eyes.

He stretches facts haphazardly
And at lying is so skillful
You know his lies are not mistakes
But are absolutely willful.

Shame on you Bill Clinton
These untruths are so outrageous
They should quarantine your tongue
Before your lying becomes contagious.

You should know the US voters
Are appalled by what you say
They voted for something different
But got conned the same old way.

Baa Baa Clinton

Baa Baa Clinton
Have you any bull?
Yes sir! Yes sir!
Three bags full!
One for the voters
One for the press
And one great big one
For the whole Congress!

Please Mr. Clinton
You can take your bull
And spread it down in Arkansas
By the big shovel full!
Because Mr. Clinton
Up North you must admit
You cannot fool the voters
Because you're full of it!

And say Mr. Clinton
You ought to know by now
You can't deny you said it
Twisting truth we don't allow
So please Mr. Clinton
Be careful what you say
The words you used a week ago
Cannot be resaid today!

Section Twelve

Law and the Courts

Court Cases

Three times in recent memory
The jury seemed to err
From what was heard on TV
The verdict wasn't fair!

But what we must consider
And to base our judgment on
Is to consider all the evidence
Before we decide the pro and con.

We also must remember
If we are not hypocrites
The jury heard the evidence
And judged the case on merits.

I know that clever lawyers
Can distort and twist the facts
But the judge who is presiding there
Should prevent unlawful acts.

Our system's not quite perfect
Sure! It may have many flaws
But what we must remember
We are a nation ruled by laws.

We tolerate dissenters
As long as they can learn
To maintain law and order
And not pillage, loot and burn.

We must accept the verdict
Because that's what law is all about
And if you do not like our system
Then get the hell on out!

Justice Denied

The balance has shifted
To the criminal's side
If retribution's delayed
And justice denied.

It's fairness we're after
The people have cried
If lawbreaking is rewarded
And justice denied.

The facts were concealed
When the witnesses lied
For truthfulness thwarted
Is justice denied.

The crooks are all laughing
When the court cannot decide
For executions delayed
Is justice denied.

The victims are suffering
And many have died
Because pity for criminals
Is justice denied.

Let's strive for correction
With fairness as guide
When criminals are punished
Justice won't be denied!

Civilized Societies

In civilized societies
Where there is commonweal
The establishment of justice
Is mankind's noblest ideal.

In nations where the rule of law
Is supreme throughout the land
The courts and all the judges
Must subscribe to the law's demand.

Yet in the thirst for vindication
Justice can often be outsmarted
By spurious claims of lawyers
Who want justice to be thwarted.

When sympathy for criminals
Exceeds the bounds of reason
Then justice is precluded
And lawbreaking is in season.

When presenting factual evidence
To the jury is denied
Sound verdicts of guilt or innocence
Is not what the system will provide.

When juries of twelve citizens
Are not given all the facts
The decisions they must render
Are little more than random acts.

When the interests of the powerful
Are given extra care and weight
The cause of equal justice
Of course! will degenerate.

When the facts are all presented
And the jury comes to a decision
Unconstitutional allegations
Should never lead to a recision.

When devious and tricky lawyers
Can distort and twist the truth
The noble cause of justice
Must be resolved in the voting booth.

If the system is not working
To protect the innocent man
Then change is necessitated
To make a more effective plan.

So if you want a system
Where the courts are ruled by laws
Then elect those legislators
Who will correct the system's flaws.

Civilized Behavior

There are sickos, psychos and such like
That should be put away for good
For those who can't control their urges
Don't belong in any neighborhood.

For if the animal urges of mankind
Are not kept in control by law
The lives of innocent people
Will succumb to fang and claw.

For no one has the right to say
"Don't hold me to the law's account"
For if one's action involves others
Then other's rights are paramount!

Every human can be trained
To control his physical desires
And learn to live as civilized
Which every society requires.

Consider The Policeman

Consider the policeman on his beat
As he ensures our safety on the street.

Consider him when his help you need
Consider him then as a friend indeed.

Consider this man who upholds the laws
And back him up in justice's cause.

All law abiding people do understand
And always follow the law's command.

Consider how laws must be enforced
That some people must always be coerced.

Now consider the policeman with his gun
And when he must use it on some one.

Consider the risk is never minimal
When he apprehends a criminal

So accept the policeman in his role
As mankind's best means of self-control.

Honor this man with his badge and gun
He's doing a job which must be done.

Section Thirteen

Tolerance

Tolerance

When I look at my fellow man
In all their great variety
It seems to take a lot of folks
To constitute society.

I see large numbers of the young
As well as middle-aged and old
But yet I find no two alike
As from a common mold.

I hear tremendous polyglot
And countless variation
Yet all are very much alike
In the human population.

When great crowds come together
And commence to push and shove
It takes a lot of tolerance
To remember brotherly love.

At times like these one's tolerance
Is put to the maximum test
For each must exercise restraint
To put up with all the rest.

On Judging People

When you see a person such as me
You can't say much for certainty
About the man I appear to be
As I stand before you physically.

For what you see is flesh and hair
But that's not me who's standing there
The real "me" is deep within
And what you see is just my skin.

The person who is really "me"
Is more complex than what you see
So judge me not on what's in view
But rather on the things I do.

For you can't tell how I may think
Or from what knowledge well I drink;
And where my thoughts originate
Or what I may expostulate.

For though you try as best you can
You cannot know your fellow man
Until you know what's in his mind
And how he views most humankind.

So if a judgment you must render
Do not think of some one's gender
For it matters not if man or woman
Just judge each person as a human.

For people wear a public face
But hold "self" in a secret place
Where deep within themselves they hide
Their real feelings and their pride.

And judge not man on what he says
With different words on different days
For words are cheap especially when
They're used to boost egos of men.

Don't be so quick to judge a man
Until you know him better than
The stranger you just chanced to meet
As you walked along the street.

For each person is made up of three
Separate terms of identity
And all three views of one should be
Looked at in there entirety.

The physical is what you see
As well as dress to some degree;
But don't judge man upon his size
Or the color of his skin or eyes.

And intellect may not reflect
One's wisdom in true retrospect
So judge not man on just his brain
When common sense is more germane.

His spirit is the best resource
To measure what a man is worth;
For you best can judge man as a whole
When you can tell what's in his soul.

For these three views together can
Complete understanding of a man
And weighed in terms of pro and con
Are what judgments should be based upon.

Oddballs

When you see someone as different
In our human populations
He must deviate from normal
Beyond three standard deviations.

The normal curve of people
Covers ninety-nine point nine percent
So for someone to be abnormal
He must be really different!

In terms of what is normal
It depends on who you are
If you think everyone is an oddball
You're not normal, you're bizarre!

Because each one of us is different
As one of many shades of gray
When you see someone as different
He is just odd in a different way!

If you think that you are normal
Just contemplate what is true
There is no other single soul
Who is exactly just like you!

So be careful judging others
Though they may seem odd it is true
When you see some one as different
The odd one may be you!

Lucky Me

When I look at my good fortune
I know I cannot boast
Its not because I'm better
I am just luckier than most.

Like when I score the most points
In the game of basketball
It is not because I'm better
I am just lucky I am tall.

And when I think of gender
Being male is what it takes
It's not because men are better
They just get more lucky breaks.

Or when I look at my white skin
I think "megalomaniac"
It's not because white is better
It's just not yellow, brown or black.

So think again you tall white man
And don't think you're so unique
You're standing where you are in life
Because you're on a lucky streak.

And don't depend on luck to keep
You at the top of fortune's ladder
For some day you will surely find
That luck simply doesn't matter.

For though you may be lucky
And receive many lucky breaks
To really get along in life
Good hard work is what it takes.

Alien From Space

As an alien from outer space
I don't understand your talk of race
You see some shading in the skin
And think it changes what's within.

You folks on earth are mighty strange
Because you vary in a narrow range,
And while minor differences there may be
You all look just alike to me.

You call each other blacks or whites
Or red or yellow; but the sights
I see when I look around the town
Are nothing more than shades of brown.

When you bleed, your blood is red
When you're killed, you're just as dead.
And you can interbreed so easily
You all blend into one humanity.

So why use words that don't make sense
And highlight each small difference
It is culture so it seems to be
That causes most diversity.

Why can't you try to see each other
As if every one is like your brother
And by increasing your familiarity
Learn to stress your great similarity.

Black Culture

The trouble with our nation's blacks
Is something that their culture lacks.
Black culture needs the kind of tools
That require people to follow rules.

They don't seem to tell their youths
They have to follow well known truths;
That all people must develop skills
So they can work and pay their bills.

Black culture ought to have a rule
That all black children go to school
And when they get their homework done
Then it's the time for having fun.

Black culture should tell teenage boys
That black girls aren't just sexual toys.
They can't be used for harmless fun
To make them pregnant, then cut and run.

Black culture should tell teenage girls
Their bodies are like precious pearls
They should not be used for sex and drugs
Or get exposed to infectious bugs.

Black women seem to have forgotten when
Black families all included men.
A man around is not a bother
And all black children need a father.

Black culture should insure that men
Become heads of households once again
And men should take the responsibility
To maintain the neighborhood in
    tranquility.

If black culture can restore these goals
And establish rightful social roles
Then each will grow in self-esteem
And all can attain the American dream.

Black culture has a lot to offer
And there really is no need to suffer.
To continue calling each one brother
They ought to stop killing one another.

L.A. Riots

The brothers are all angry
And are rioting they say
Because they've seen injustice
On the streets in old L.A.

It seems there was a black man
Who was beat up by the cops
And the brothers will keep rioting
Until this injustice stops.

The mayor even said so
It was a breakdown of the law
When white cops beat up a black man
And that's what everybody saw.

They showed it there on TV
And it was plain as day and night
The black man lying on the ground
And all the cops were white.

Yeah! Sure they had a trial
And went through all the paces
But the process didn't help at all
To maintain peace among the races.

You're damn right we're mad as hell
And we won't take it any more
Because now we've seen it on TV
They can't deny it like before.

For black men, justice isn't fair
Or that's the way it seems
We never seem to get the breaks
When we try to reach our dreams.

How come we're the ones to suffer?
How come we can't get good jobs?
'Cause that's why we're on welfare
And that's why the black man robs.

If we had better housing
And jobs where the pay was good
We would be better citizens
And protect the neighborhood.

We would run out all the dopers
And chase all the gangs away
So our children would be safe at home,
On the streets and where they play.

We'd make our children stay in school
And do their homework too,
So they'd keep out of trouble
And have constructive things to do.

And then there's having babies
By girls still in their teens
If they had jobs and husbands
There would be no welfare queens.

If black men all had steady jobs
And could support their wives
They'd all stay out of trouble
And live respectable quiet lives.

I know we bring it on ourselves
By taking drink and dope
But that's what happens everywhere
When you've given up on hope.

I know black girls get pregnant
By black boys and their friends
But they have little hope in life
On which self-respect depends.

So pay attention Whitey!
And heed what's happening here
'Cause we demand a share of the future
And we want justice everywhere.

Peace Needs

The sun has set
With great regret
On a fact which is conclusive
That men of war
Keep fighting for
A peace which is elusive.

Those men of steel
Will always feel
They must settle things by fighting
Though it is wise
To compromise
Waging war is more exciting.

To obtain peace
These wars must cease
All men must learn toleration
And not to fight
For every slight
But forgive each provocation.

For peace to last
Forget the past!
And look forward to tranquility
And strive to make
For your children's sake
A future based on civility!

Section Fourteen

Anti-Abortion Poems

Legalized Abortion

Sound the siren loud and long
Something in the world is wrong
When unborn children live in fear
Since legalized abortion's here.

For by decree of the highest court
Pregnant women can now abort
Lives of their young they'll never see
And call it the "right for privacy."

Righteous people are appalled
At this modern Buchenwald
And shame is felt throughout the land
For these abortion murders on demand.

So call the doctor with his knife
To come and end that helpless life
Without any feeling or sentiment
But because a birth is inconvenient.

Does the doctor wear a hangman's hood
When he sheds that innocent blood?
Does he brag about his skill
And how proficiently he can kill?

And what say you about the nurse
Whose gentle hand is now a curse?
Do her hands have a soothing feel
When she helps to kill instead of heal?

Do other patients cringe in fear
When they see her coming near?
Has her compassion for the ill
Changed into the urge to kill?

And what kind of mother is this woman
Whose heart of stone is so inhuman
That with heartless, cold and tearless eye
She wants her unborn child to die.

How can children love this mother
After she has killed their brother?
Can they ever hug and kiss her
After she has slain their sister?

What kind of beast is this child's father
Who calls his own child such a bother
That with great relief he gladly pays
To end his offspring's hapless days?

What kind of animal is this man
Who promotes and cheers this evil plan
To kill his child and so abort
The need to provide the child's support?

And hear those advocates loud and shrill
Who demand they have the right to kill
And claim they have the right to choose
Which child shall die without excuse.

And hear that hypocritical politician
Whose morally feeble illogical position
Is that murder is wrong as a personal view
But perfectly all right for others to do.

What kind of ghouls are so sadistic
That they can cheer at each statistic
That shows the score of this abomination
Of murdering children to control population?

Who can be secure in such a nation
With such a degraded civilization
That murder is done by government dictums
Of helpless children as the primary victims.

Surely this is a depraved society
Whose values are warped beyond propriety
When felons lives are saved as precious
But unborn children are called pernicious.

We pray Oh God! hold back thy wrath
Against these people on the path
Of widespread murder and extermination
Of these unborn children of thy creation.

And may heaven hear this sad lament
For these babes so innocent.
May angels weep and may angels mourn
For these unloved, unwanted and unborn.

Unwanted Children

It used to be in old Shanghai
Unwanted children were exposed to die
While in Thailand, kids are good as gold
When money's needed, one is sold.

In the USA, we do the same
But we call it by a different name.
If the unborn baby's mother wills it
An abortion doctor simply kills it.

In America here, we think it's neat
To treat dead fetuses like meat.
We harvest "tissue" for the lab
And have "Research" pick up the tab.

We use the parts that may evoke
A good response in older folk.
We claim that this is like triage
And unused parts are just garbage.

You say we have a different basis
Then tell me what the moral case is.
Why does age have any bearing
When one's involved in child rearing.

Morally, if it's all right to kill them
Why should it be so bad to sell them?
Can you say with complete confidence
That there really is a moral difference?

Oh God! We hope one of heaven's goals
Is to save and love these little souls.

Child Slaughter

Freedom of choice is not defensible
Killing children is reprehensible
Because it's just impossible to assume
A child's not alive in the mother's womb.

They say these unborns have no worth
And too many children clutter Earth.
Remember Hitler used a similar ruse
And used it to get rid of Jews!

Freedom of choicers thus excuse
Killing the ones the mothers choose
As being too much trouble to
Care and tend for like others do.

They say they have the right of choice
Since the unborn child has no voice
They kill the ones that appear to be
A drain upon their luxury.

When the heart is heard in the stethoscope
The little heart beat signals hope
That if the womb is not defiled
That heartbeat will become a child!

So do not claim the fetus class
Is just a parasitic mass
That can be excised by a knife
Because it never was a human life.

The child is not a parasite
It is alive by God-given right
And whether it is son or daughter
Abortion is always child slaughter.

For every unwanted child's conception
(And their should never be exception)
If the child's life must be aborted
The father's sex drive must be thwarted.

For fathers should be made to bear
The blame for pregnancies where
The unborn child is hated so
It must be killed so it won't grow.

For if the father is held accountable
The facts will soon be insurmountable
That no unwanted children will be sired
And irresponsible fathers not admired!

But sad to say there is exception
To nature's joy at each conception
For society never can endorse
The father's use of physical force.

If at this sad time the innocent child
Is sacrificed as somehow defiled
In retribution for this atrocity
Society must demand reciprocity.

For if the fetus must be lost
The responsible father must suffer cost
This guilty rapist should be locked away
And lose his manhood on the way.

Hey Mom! It's Me!

Hey Mom! It's me in here
I am growing big and strong
I am looking forward to my birth
And now it won't be long!

Hey Mom! I want a chance to grow
I want a chance to live and show
You what a blessing I can be
I want to make you proud of me!

Hey Mom! I want a chance to see
Your happy face smiling down at me.
I want to feel your loving arm
Holding me all snug and warm!

Hey Mom! Can't you hear? It's me!
If you will only let things be
I have lots of love to give
If you will only let me live!

Mom! Don't go to that murder mill!
Mom! It's little me they want to kill!
Don't let them tear my flesh apart!
Don't let them stop my beating heart!

Mom! Don't let them take me from your womb
And put me directly in the tomb!
Or what is worse just cut and slash
And throw my body in the trash!

MOM! MOM!...
And then all is silence
Except the sucking sound of the vacuum
As the now dead fetus is removed..........

SECTION FIFTEEN

Seasonal Poems

Springtime

When daylight time grows longer
And winter cold and snow recedes
The promise of warmer weather
Is what every summer-lover needs.

When balmy southern breezes
Begin to thaw the frozen earth
The stirring of the dormant sap
Shows it's time for life's rebirth.

When the sun is rising higher
And it's rays grow more intense
You can feel the change that's coming
And respond with every sense.

When trees begin to blossom
And the bees begin to hum
You can cast off winter's doldrums
Because the time for spring has come.

Faun and flora are awaiting
For this magic time they share
When rebirth is universal
And new life is everywhere.

Springtime is so magnificent
The whole world wants to sing
Because everyone is happy
When winter turns to spring.

Summer Envy

I see the white and fleecy clouds
Adrift on summer breeze
They seem to have no cares at all
And go where e'er they please.

They float in airy space so free
Above the earth unbound
Like dabs of downy cotton balls
Within the blue surround.

Would I were so unfettered
And would I were so free
I, too, would spend my summer days
Just drifting leisurely.

But I have made commitments
To many earth-bound folk
So dreams of carefree drifting
Are naught but wisps of smoke.

I've made too many promises
To people that I love
Thus I cannot shirk my duty
And drift like clouds above.

Since I have responsibilities
And goals that beckon me
I can't go drifting off in space
Or live life aimlessly

September

In September
I remember
It's time for going back to school
How I dread it
Now I've said it
I don't like this grownup rule!

Foot steps dragging
Spirit sagging
Carefree days are now no more
Getting ready
Slow and steady
Kissing mother at the door.

Old friends meeting
Gleeful greeting
Classmates who have been away.
Seat assignment
Then confinement
On this first most dreadful day.

Lesson learning
Eyes are burning
Reading 'bout some ancient wars
Mind can wander
Way out yonder
Wishing I was out-of-doors.

End of summer
What a bummer
Yearning to be grown up too
'Twill be sublime
To spend the time
Doing things that grownups do!

Comes October

Comes October
The days grow shorter
And the sun has lost its searing heat;
The birds stop singing and fly away;
Flowers wither and turn to seed;
Leaves turn color, fall and blow away.
Comes October the year is winding down.

Comes October
It is time to harvest grapes and corn and apples.
The labor of growing things
Now yield the bounty of nature.
The tiller reaps the rich rewards of spring plowing
And summer weeding and watering in the hot sun.
Comes October, it's time to reap the fruit of
one's labor.

Comes October,
The elderly retire from their life's occupation
So the rewards of life's labor can be enjoyed.
The preparation time of youth
And the long drudging hours on the job
Now yield the precious pension.
Although the days grow short and cold creeps in
The bones creak and the muscles grow stiff
These are the golden years.
Comes October
One's life is winding down.

Christmas Anticipation

At Christmastime when all are feeling grand
And everyone shows signs of brotherhood
The Christmas lights are lit around the land
To help people get in the Christmas mood.
The children all anticipate the day
For all the songs they hear have Christmas themes
They know that good behavior is the way
For Santa to fulfill their wishful dreams,
The stores all seem to have a festive air
To help create the look of happiness.
The harried shoppers do not seem to care
That Christmas also causes budget stress.
Anticipation seems to be the way
To make the whole world happy Christmas
Day!

Christmas Time

Christmas is the time for sharing
And for giving gifts and such,
Christmas is the time for mem'ries
And for friends to keep in touch.

Christmas is the time for parties
For making toasts and having cheer.
Christmas is the time for feasting
For it's the happy time of year.

Christmas is the time for praying
And remembering a baby's birth.
Christmas means forgiving others
And for promoting Peace On Earth.

So let's join hands and pray together
And raise our voices as we sing
***Gloria in Excelsis Deo**
And Deo Gratias for everything!

Old Bones

Old Bones hates winters
Because winter makes Old Bones suffer.
Cold slows the blood and stiffens joints.
In winter Old Bones wears longjohns
Puts on wool clothing
And wraps up in warm blankets.
In winter, Old Bones stays indoors
Turns the thermostat way up
And yearns for summer.

In spring, Old Bones takes heart
And knows that the warm sun
Will chase away the chill of winter.
In the spring, Old Bones
Looks for sunny places to sit
And wonders why spring is so late.
Even though the trees are in blossom
And the flowers and bushes are in bloom
Old Bones still shivers a lot.

In summer, Old Bones comes alive again.
He opens all the windows
And doesn't mind sitting in a breeze.
For Old Bones enjoys the summer sun
Because it seldom gets too warm
For Old Bones.
The warmth seems to oil old joints
And the humidity lubricates the skin.
Summer is kind to Old Bones.

Then the first cool evening in the fall
Sends chills into Old Bones
Because he dreads the end of summer.
But Old Bones rejoices
In those last few sunny autumn days
Which are more like summer than winter.
Then Old Bones can forget for awhile
That the next season is winter
Because Old Bones hates winters.

Section Sixteen

Nursery Rhyme Parodies

Little Miss Muffet

Little Miss Muffet
Sat on a tuffet
At the beauty contest to rest for a minute.
Although she was cute
She wasn't a beaut
So was fearful that she wouldn't win it.

To increase her appeal
She prepared a fine meal
And invited the judges to dinner.
The food was so good
It put them in the mood
To declare Miss Muffet the winner.

The other girls cried, "Foul"
And put up a big howl
When the judges announced their decision.
But Miss Muffet knew
What the judges would do
Because her dinner had biased their vision.

Now she wears the crown
Has the fame and renown
For she was elected queen of them all.
Though the other girls hate her
They still want her to cater
The food for the next debutante's ball!

Little Bo Peep

Little Bo Peep just lost her sheep
When she didn't pay them attention
They started to roam
And couldn't find their way home
But leaving home was not their intention.

Little Bo Peep must look for her sheep
She can't see them from where she is sitting
It's time for the shearing
Of the coat they are wearing
And she does need the wool for her knitting.

When little Bo Peep couldn't find her sheep
She had to go see a lawyer
She expected a fleecing
Because his fee kept increasing
Before she even got out of the foyer.

He found the sheep for little Bo Peep
But left her nary a button
Now Bo Peep is sad
Since she lost all she had
While the lawyer is dining on mutton.

But little Bo Peep can save her sheep
And doesn't even have to mind them
She can keep them you see
In her own memory
So she'll always know where to find them.

Little Boy Blue

Our Little Boy Blue left us to blow his horn
The band needed a trumpet to blow until morn
They didn't care if his pants were ragged and torn
Or that his unruly hair was long and unshorn.
We knew he was addicted to cocaine and porn
Because we had loved him from the day he was born.

We remember the time his young fancy took flight
When blowing his horn was his greatest delight.
He was just seventeen and his horn was just right
To give self-expression to his artistic birthright.
So great was his promise and future so bright
He practiced his blowing from morn until night.

He blew on his trumpet all the latest hot licks
Before he gave in to his great need for a fix.
He enjoyed the weird places where he got his kicks
But his candle was burning with multiple wicks.
He ignored all our warnings because we were hicks
But Nature's not fooled by young men's sly tricks.

There came the sad day when he could not come back
For a body can't work when the drugs interact.
Tho all of his nerves were flying high from the crack
He still wanted to try to run wild with the pack.
When his poor heart at last succumbed to an attack
They buried his remains in the coroner's sack.

We say sadly good-bye to our Little Boy Blue
Whose dreams were so many, but his days were so few.
His music was divine on the horn that he blew
But the drugs did him in as the drugs often do.
We continue on living as the living have to
But there's ache in our heart for our Little Boy Blue.

Old King Cole

Old King Cole
Was a merry old soul
Until his kingdom ran out of money
The citizens guffawed
Tee heed and ha hawed
But the king didn't think it was funny.

Since Ole King Cole
Wanted gold in his bowl
The peasants were asked to provide it
He said, "It's not greed
For the gold that I need."
But his subjects all found ways to hide it.

So Ole King Cole
To get out of the hole
Raised the taxes on everyone's income
The peasants all yelled
And said, "We've rebelled."
And rioted all over the kingdom.

Then Ole King Cole
Took a loyalty poll
But the results that he found so upset him
That he and his wife
Had to flee for their life
Because the vote had been to behead him!

Now Ole King Cole
Has to live on the dole
And his pipe and his bowl are empty.
Instead of a crown
All he wears is a frown
And he's no longer part of the gentry.

Poor Old King Cole
Is a sorry old soul
For his kingdom is all but forgotten
He just sits on his butt
In a ramshackle hut
And is miffed by the fix he has got in.

The Golden Fleece

Mary had a little lamb
That had a golden fleece
And everywhere that Mary went
People asked her for a piece!

So Mary kept her lamb at home
To keep it safe from harm
And when she sheared her little lamb
She had the gold to keep her warm.

Little Jack Horner

Little Jack Horner
Had to sit on the corner
For telling his mother a lie!
It made her so sad
That Jack had been bad
She almost started to cry!

Then Little Jack Horner
Said from his corner,
"I'm sorry for causing you pain
If you let me go
I want you to know
I will never tell lies again."

But Jack in his corner
Intended to scorn her
Because he didn't mean what he said.
If he ever got caught
The next time he ought
To not lie but just shake his head.

But still Mother Horner
Kept Jack in the corner
To teach him to tell the truth
But to no one's surprise
Her fibs and white lies
Set a poor example for youth.

Jack Be Nimble

Jack be nimble, Jack be quick
The team needs you at Candlestick!

We need one run to tie the score
To win the game we need two more!

It's the top of the ninth and all are tense
The ball must be hit out over the fence.

Our Jack can do it without a doubt
He's the only sub left with homerun clout.

Go for it Jack and make your mark!
So Jack hit the ball clear out of the park.

Our Jack is the hero, he's the homerun king
He's sure to be back at the 'Stick next
spring.

Harry the Fairy

Harry the Fairy
Was very contrary
And sometimes he was bad
He put ants in the pants
Of Dwayne the Dwarf
And made Dwayne awfully mad!

So Dwayne the Dwarf
Went down to the wharf
And caught a fish that stings
He took out the stinger
With his thumb and his finger
And stuck it on Harry's wings!

Then Harry the Fairy
Wasn't nearly as merry
His wings hurt when he tried to use them
So he said to Dwayne,
"I won't do it again."
But Dwayne refused to excuse him!

Then Bridget the Midget
Said, "Perhaps if you fidget
The stinger will come out by itself!"
So Harry squirmed all about
Until the stinger came out
And he put it up high on a shelf!

But Elvin the Elf
Lived up there on the shelf
And he didn't like that at all
For the stinger up there
Could get caught in his hair
And he was very afraid it would fall!

So then he called Dwayne
To come get it again
To take it back to the ocean
So Dwayne put a chain
On the end of a cane
And removed it without a commotion.

Now Dwayne isn't mad
And Harry's not bad
And Bridget and Elvin are friends
They have learned what is best
Is to be good to the rest
And if you hurt someone; quick make
amends!

So Harry the Fairy
Is no longer contrary
And he treats everyone very well
They all love one another
And play nicely together
In places where small people dwell!

The Wicked Old Witch

There was an old woman
    who lived in an attic
She wasn't quite crazy
    But she sure was erratic.

She chased away children
    with a willow tree switch
That's why they all called her
    The wicked old witch!

She lived alone in her attic
    and raised big ugly rats
While her only companions
    were spiders and bats.

She collected old cobwebs,
    toad stools and nettles
Then cooked them together
    in some old copper kettles.

She brewed magical potions
    and sold them for money
What these potions could do to you
    Sure wasn't funny.

She could change little girls
    into fuzzy white rabbits
Especially those girls who had
    lots of bad habits.

She could make turtles and lizards
Out of bad little boys
Especially those wicked ones
who made too much noise.

She would stay home all day
and go out at night
And sneak up on people
To give them a big fright.

The townspeople all tried
to make her go away
But she couldn't be expelled
or chased out so they say.

Then one day they found her
Lying drowned in a ditch
And that was sadly the end of
the wicked old witch.

Section Seventeen

Miscellaneous

In Memory's Eye

In memory's eye, a once seen view
Can be recalled and seen anew
A picture too, remains at hand
To view again at thought's command.

In memory's ear, a once heard sound
Is stored forever to resound.
A voice in memory's storage bin
Needs but a thought to speak again.

In memory's finger tip, a touch
Once made and felt is stored as such.
A thought recalls the touch and more
And tells me what I touched before.

In memory's book, the printed word
Is recalled again and even heard.
The words are there for me to see
They're silent, yet they speak to me.

These images are quite profuse
They're ready there for me to use
So when I want to think a thought
I check to see what memory's got.

The thoughts are dormant and confined
They're dead and buried in my mind
But when I recall them for review
They all spring back to life anew.

Children's Laughter

While sitting on a park bench
Tending all my children grand
I can hear their innocent laughter
While they dig dogholes in the sand.

Oh! Childhood is a happy time
And its pleasures are well known
Because the joyfulness of children
Has an enchantment all its own.

But too soon it will be over
Too soon will age contend
And the time of childish laughter
Will too soon be at end.

For from the vantage of the aged
I can see their life unfold
And the loss of childish pleasures
Is too painful to behold.

But as one ponders childhood
And mourns its meager span
One can see the need for passage
In the cycle life of man.

For though we earnestly desire
To keep everything at its prime
We cannot stop life's progression
Nor hold back the pass of time.

My Brother

Of all the people God has made
To live with one another,
He never made a finer man
Than when he made my brother.

We were fairly close in age
And were the best of friends,
Whenever we had a falling out
We were quick to make amends.

Of course, we had our minor fights
For ego self asserting
But never once in all our tears
Did there occur a hurting.

To me he was a trusted pal
And I've never found another.
He was always there to champion me
Because he was my big brother.

If all the nations in this world
Could find this same relation
I'm sure that lasting peace would reign
Among every brother nation.

If every man would only trust
And see every man as brother,
This would surely be a peaceful world
'Cause we would all love one another.

My Coronary

Here I lie upon my back
A victim of a heart attack.
The Doctor's come to lead the fight
And help my heart keep beating right.
The probes are in, the sensors glow
To tell the Doc what he needs to know.
The "IVs" shed their tears of balm
To help and heal and keep me calm.
The nurses with their loving care
Can comfort me most everywhere.

The prayers of friends have all been said
To add to mine for divine aid
And now dear God, it is plain to see
The help I need must come from thee.
I'm near death's door, I see the pit
PLEASE GOD DON'T LET ME FALL IN IT.
Into thy hands, Oh Lord, I pray
Have "ICU" place me there today.
Then grip me tight, I pray Oh Lord,
Not just for now but afterward.

~ ~ ~

My feet are back on solid ground
My heart once more secure and sound.
My thanks are due to a great many
I hope I've not forgotten any.
Thank you Doctor for your skill
There is no doubt I'll pay your bill.

Thank you nurses in many ways
I'll gladly vote for a new pay raise.
And thank you staff for all you do
May you receive a pay raise too.

And thank you friends for all your prayers
Tell others that He'll answer theirs.
But Oh Dear God! on bended knee
Most of my thanks must go to Thee
I thank Thee for these extra days
To do Thy will and sing Thy praise.
I thank Thee for these added hours
For the added music and added flowers.
Lord, guide my life from here on out
For love of Thee is what it is all about.

Nature's Beauty

It takes all the mighty oceans
It takes all the solid land
To make our precious planet
So beautiful and grand.

On every mighty mountain
On every plot of ground
On every single place on earth
There's beauty to be found.

Take all the lovely rivers
And every lake and stream
When added all together
Nature's beauty is supreme.

So when you visit nature
To enjoy the rural scene
Lend a hand to Mother Nature
And help keep our planet clean.

For nature is for everyone
And not for just a few
And protecting Mother Nature
Is what everyone must do.

Sonoma Wine Country

In the valley by the river
Where the air is fresh and clean
You can see the grapes agrowing
On the vines so lush and green.

The redwoods on the hillsides
Add a splendor all their own
To enhance the fertile valley
Where the premium grapes are grown.

The various soil conditions
Found in this locality
Give the grapes a special flavor
And the wine an unique quality.

The climate is perfection
And stimulates the growing vines
To produce the lushest grapes of all
From which to make the finest wines.

Then when the grapes are ready
And are hanging ripe and red
The harvest crush is hectic
Until the juice is put to bed.

The winemaker is the master.
He watches all with practiced eye
He guards fermenting with his life
And the taste will tell you why.

The juice is fermented slowly
In casks of oaken wood
The ambient temperature is controlled
To make sure the flavor's good.

He ages wine with patience
Then he bottles it with care
And affixes his private label
For shipping everywhere.

You may sip this wine at leisure
Or drink it with a meal
It will enhance your love of life
By the way it makes you feel.

You may like the Zinfandel
The Chenin Blanc or Beaujolais
Or feast your tongue with Merlot
White Chablis or Red Gamay.

So drink a glass of vino!
Smell the aroma and bouquet
Then taste the fruity flavor
And your blues will fade away!

My Pets

I have a bird named Tweety
She is so very pretty
But when she won't sing sweetly
    It makes me want to cry!

I have a fish named Goldie
She swims around so boldly
But looks at me so coldly
    It makes me want to cry!

I've got a dog named Barry
His coat is long and hairy
But he's too big for me to carry
    So it makes me want to cry!

I've got a cat named Tabby
Who always seems so crabby
She scratches when I pick her up
    So it makes me want to cry!

I love all my little friends
I keep them all inside their pens
And I know that none of them intends
    To make me want to cry!

I wish that I could find a way
So all my pets and I could play
Then we could be happy every day
    So then I'd never have to cry!

Plant a Tree

There are those who seem to think
That trees are just about extinct.
They say to loggers, "You must cease
From cutting down our full grown trees."

"Or soon there wont be trees to show
Our children how the forests grow.
For children have the right to see
The grandeur of a living tree."

To those doomsayers I voice a plea
For our children's sake go plant a tree.
And instead of voicing such dismay
Start planting trees this very day.

And trees are easy enough to plant
You can plant them anywhere you want.
Just put a seedling in the ground
And watch it grow up tall and sound.

Trees don't take a lot of care
Since they will grow 'most everywhere.
Just add some water and by-and-by
That tree will reach up to the sky.

So be one of the thoughtful folk
Just dig a hole and plant an oak.
And stop this everlasting whine
Go find a spot and plant a pine.

So if it's woods you're looking for
Go out and plant a sycamore.
And if you want the air more robust
Buy a seedling and plant a locust.

And let's plant trees in every space
So trees are growing every place.
Then we can leave to posterity
Great forests as our legacy.

In Memory of Dad

O dear God listen to my plea
Grant to our Dad eternity.
Dear God, we beg thee hear our prayer
Take him up to heaven there.
And God, accept his humble soul.
Grant him heaven as his goal
For we were all the world he had
So God, have mercy on our Dad.

He spent his life for us alone
Now for his sins let us atone.
For our neglect he paid a price
Though his life was one of sacrifice.
His life was one of work and pain
Surcease from toil he never gained
For us, he gave the life he had
So God, shed blessings on our Dad.

From his example may we learn
The righteous way is the way to turn.
We have learned from what he said
Now may we follow where he led.
He taught the things we had to know
He showed us all the way to go.
He gave us all the love he had
So God, provide a good place for our Dad.

Bernard Yaeger was born in the sandhills of Nebraska, was raised in the snows of Minnesota, and attended the University of Iowa and Purdue. He received a BA and an MS in Psychology and developed into a Human Factor Design Engineer. He spent twenty-eight years with the Honeywell Corp.

Unlike Poe, the author's first priority was supporting and educating his family of five children all of whom graduated from various University of California campuses. Three children went on to advanced degrees, an MBA, an MD, and a PhD in Economics.

The author first encountered poetry in a high school English class and wrote poems on and off during his working years. In retirement, his interest in poetry was rekindled by reading and studying poetry and books on poetry. He joined the "Poets of the Vineyard" which is a group of poets of all persuasions who meet monthly for readarounds of their material. The advice, criticisms, corrections, and suggestions of the group were especially helpful in encouraging the author to continue writing.

To order additional books, please use coupon below.

Mail or fax to:

Brunswick Publishing Corporation

1386 LAWRENCEVILLE PLANK ROAD
LAWRENCEVILLE, VIRGINIA 23868
Tel: 804-848-3865 • Fax: 804-848-0607
www.brunswickbooks.com

Order Form

___ copy (s) of ***My Vice Is Verses*** by Bernard Yaeger
$12.95 ea., paperback .... $ ____________

Total, books .... $ ____________
VA residents add 4.5% sales tax .... $ ____________
Shipping – within U.S. and Canada
$4.50 1st copy .... $ ____________
$.50 ea. additional copy .... $ ____________

Total .... $ ____________

❑ Check enclosed.

❑ Charge to my credit card:
❑ VISA ❑ MasterCard ❑ American Express

Card #______________________________ Exp. Date __________

Signature: ______________________________________

Name ______________________________________

Address ______________________________________

City______________________________ State______ Zip ___________

Phone # ______________________________________